TheWord Mindset

An imprint of The Word Mindset

Website: www.thewordmindset.com
rajulajacobchandran@gmail.com

First published in the United States of America by
The Word Mindset 2024

Cover & Book design: Rajkumar Jacob
radicaljacob@gmail.com

ISBN 979-8-218-42610-1

"You will know the truth, and
the truth will make you free."
John 8:32

✻✻✻

"To become mightily empowered
through the Spirit of God in
the inner man."
Ephesians 3:16

✻✻✻

Jesus answered, " Love the Lord
your God with all your heart,
all your soul, and all your mind."
Matthew 22:37

✻✻✻

DEDICATION

To my Mother, who never stopped believing in me.

To my mentor Dr. Leonard Abraham, who planted the seed of God's truth in my mind and persuaded me to write.

To all of my destiny helpers who reminded me that the Word of God has the power to change me.

ACKNOWLEDGMENTS

I benefitted heavily from the support of my family and friends during the creation of this book. I would like to take this opportunity to thank Dr. Leonard Abraham, Mantle of Elijah Ministries, for his enthusiastic support and encouragement to write this book. My son, Jacob Chandran has made my writing a complete joy and has been a pillar of support in the writing of this book. Jacob's input, thoughts and meticulous feedback have been a great inspiration in my journey to write this book. My sincere thanks to my daughter Evangeline Deepa Chandran for taking the time and effort to edit and offer insightful observations. Thanks to Amanda Kim and Jeanine McLaughlin for editing this book.

I am deeply grateful to my brother Rajkumar Jacob for his valuable time and effort in formatting, designing and printing this book.

Finally, I am thankful to my husband, Suresh Chandran, for the support and encouragement throughout this project. This book would not have been possible without his support in my faith journey.

My passion is about developing a faith mindset, and it has helped me to grow in my faith journey. It is my sincere wish and prayer that it will do the same for you.

CONTENTS

Section 1: Principles

Principles are fundamental values, rules, and habits
that provide a foundation for life. They are basic
qualities that motivate action.

Section 2: Disciplines

Disciplines are orderly patterns of behavior that
enable us to think and work effectively.

Section 3: Guidelines and Process

Processes are a series of actions and guidelines
that make us more effective in our way of living,
thinking and feeling.

Be empowered
to live an authentic
inner-directed life,
guided by deep truths
in the Bible.

INTRODUCTION

HOW YOU WILL BENEFIT FROM THIS BOOK

This book is about becoming empowered to live an authentic inner-directed life, guided by deep truths in the Bible rather, than external influences to conform.

A mindset is a set of attitudes, beliefs, and thought patterns that shape one's worldview and actions. A 'Faith Mindset' provides a firm foundation that is based on biblical principles, disciplines, guidelines and processes. There is a purpose for each aspect of the faith mindset:

The Principles -The principles are fundamental values, rules, and habits that provide a foundation for life. They are basic qualities that motivate action.

The Disciplines - The disciplines are a collection of promises and behaviors from the Bible that empower the inner person.

Processes - The processes are a series of actions or guidelines that make us more effective in our way of living, thinking and feeling.

Faith is the backbone of the biblical worldview and will last for a lifetime. The Bible says in Romans 8: 5–8: "For those who live according to the body set their minds on the things of the body [which gratify the body], but those who live according to the Spirit, set their minds on the things of the Spirit [God's will and purpose]." (AMP)

The idea of the 'Faith Mindset' emerged from my journey in living out the Christian faith and my experience in Project Management.

Project Management is the application of principles, disciplines and processes to achieve specific objectives through a project life cycle, within the constraints of goals, cost and time. Similarly, a faith mindset is the application of biblical principles, disciplines and processes to achieve specific objectives and purposes through the various phases of our life, within the constraints of body, mind, heart and spirit.

Having a faith mindset can have profound effects on our life. Through the faith mindset, we can draw on an inner strength that no one can take away.

In this book, I will show you how to embrace "deep truths" in the Bible and apply them to your practical everyday life. This process of creating outer change via inner change is fundamental to the Christian life. The Word permeates through every part of a person's life, from the mundane to the grandiose. A faith mindset offers the raw material to live to your full potential and towards your God-given destiny. It affects your destiny, worldview, perspective, resilience, and much more.

It is my privilege to share my collection of "nuggets of deep truth" from my faith journey. Each chapter begins with a question followed by my response. I have added scriptural references throughout the content, so that you can see the faith mindset in action. I will show you small ways to apply these "nuggets of deep truth," so that you can recognize the mindset that is guiding your life, why it is relevant, and how it works in real life.

It is important to start small. Starting small enables us to build the confidence needed for bigger challenges. The Bible says, 'do not despise the day of small beginnings' (Zechariah 4:10).

WHY I WROTE THIS BOOK

ABOUT THE AUTHOR

This book is about my discovery of faith as part of my journey from Chennai (also known as Madras), in Tamil Nadu, India to the East Coast of the United States. I did not have a religious upbringing and had no clue what the Bible was or who Jesus Christ was until someone gifted me a Bible in high school. I was seeking answers to many questions and searching for meaning in various places. What I read in the gospel of John intrigued me, and thus began my journey to investigate the Bible. I tried to practice and test what I read in the Bible in my everyday life.

As I began to test the authenticity of biblical principles in my daily life, I started to experience fulfillment in my search for meaning and purpose. I began to ask more questions and find more answers. My faith in Jesus Christ was becoming a game changer. I began to embrace and cultivate biblical disciplines for everyday living. Since then, I have never regretted my faith journey with Christ.

Faith has been a driving force throughout my journey through life; it has become a beacon of light and blazing fire within me as I tried to navigate through the challenges of life.

This book is the outcome of the deep longing and fire within me to express my faith journey in writing. My urge to write this book emerged as I began publishing articles for the Mantle of Elijah magazine, under the leadership of Dr. Leonard Abraham. He inspired me to compile my articles into a book. With the help of destiny helpers, I was able to turn my deep longing into a reality.

It is no exaggeration to say this book would not have come to fruition without the support and encouragement of my son Jacob Chandran, who has been my unfailing champion to write, edit, and publish this work. I want to thank my daughter Evangeline Chandran for her constructive criticism and skills in editing my writing. My sincere thanks to Amanda Kim and Jenine Mclaughlin for editing this book. I am greatly indebted to my husband Suresh Chandran for standing by me through this long journey. Last but not the least, I am deeply grateful to my brother Rajkumar Jacob for working tirelessly on the formatting, designing and publishing of this book.

This book encapsulates over 40 years of my experience in cultivating a faith-based mindset in my personal and working life. My journey began in Chennai, India where I grew up as one of five children. My father passed away when I was very young and suddenly, we were thrown into a life of financial, emotional, and spiritual hardship. Friends and well-wishers shared the Bible with my mother, Rajeswari Roopsingh, as an expression of hope in the midst of hopelessness. She put her faith in Christ and it changed her life. Slowly but surely, it also started to change life for each of her five children. By reading the gospel of John in the Bible in the privacy of my home, I was able to find answers to my quest for purpose and meaning to life. God's word changed my worldview and continues to change it every day. I have never regretted my decision to put my faith in Christ.

In high school and college, I began to get involved with various student groups at Stella Maris college, Adyar House of Prayer (HOP) youth group, Union of Evangelical Students of India (UESI), and Navodaya team, which furthered strengthened my faith. My faith continued to grow as I immersed myself in playing basketball for my high school team at Kendriya Vidyalaya I.I.T

(KVIIT), my college team at Stella Maris college, Madras University, and Tamilnadu State. These diverse experiences further reinforced my faith as I was able to apply and execute my faith in my daily life.

Even though daily living was a struggle, my mother held on to her faith in Jesus Christ, and that propelled her to walk by faith, and not by sight. She encouraged me to apply for further studies abroad in the United States of America (USA). I received a fellowship to pursue my Graduate studies at Southern Illinois University in the USA. The rest is history. After completing graduate school in Illinois, I continued my studies in the Baltimore, Maryland area and married Suresh Chandran. After teaching at a community college, I then took up a job at Allied Irish Bank (AIB), later called M&T Bank in Baltimore, Maryland. I represented the AIB USA Women's Basketball team at the AIB championship in Dublin, Ireland.

I began to grow and develop professionally as well. With certification as a Project Management Professional, and Federal Acquisition Certification for Program and Project Managers, I started to progress and advance in my project management career. I have been working for over 30 years: 10 years in the private industry and 20 years in public service. I currently work as a Senior Project Manager on the east coast of the USA. We have two children Evangeline and Jacob.

This book is broken down into principles, disciplines, and processes similar to project management. I chose this approach because of my experience, knowledge and skills in Project Management for nearly three decades. Project management is the application of principles, disciplines and processes to achieve specific objectives while working within scope, budget and schedule constraints. The principles provide a foundation for faith-based mindset. The disciplines are a collection of behaviors that enable us to be empowered by God's truth. The processes are guidelines to be more effective in our way of living.

A faith-based mindset is a habit and a way of life that is built upon Biblical principles, disciplines and processes. A mindset that is based on faith needs to be understood and lived daily through the Word of God. By harnessing a faith-based mindset, it is possible to transform one's personal and eternal destiny.

My faith journey has spanned over 40 years. In that time, I have cultivated a faith-based approach to life. My desire is that by reading this book, you too will be empowered to cultivate a faith-based mindset and execute it.

PRINCIPLES

The principles are fundamental values, rules, and habits that provide a foundation for life. They are basic qualities that motivate action.

What do we
know when
we read in the
Bible that
we have been
created in the
image of God?
Is this a
unique relation
between God
and humanity?

Chapter 1

Creation Mandate

Image: a reproduction or imitation of the form of a person or thing

A mandate is a commission to do something, an order or authority to act in a certain way. The mandate in creation says that humanity is created in God's image (Genesis 1:1-3), and that God has equipped humanity to live according to that image (Genesis 2:4-25, Romans 1:20).

The dictionary defines an image as 'a visual representation of something'. It has its roots in the Latin word imitari, meaning 'to copy or imitate'. In Greek, image means an icon, likeness, or picture.

Image versus Likeness
In Hebrew, the phrase 'image of God' istzelem Elohim, translated as 'likeness', and is derived from the root word 'shadow'. We are like the shadows God casts on the world. "The yearning to know what cannot be known, to comprehend the incomprehensible, to touch and taste the unapproachable, arises from the image of God in the nature of man and woman" (A.W. Tozer, *The Knowledge of the Holy*).

In the Bible, the image of God applies uniquely to humans. The image of God is symbolic of the relationship between God and humanity.

The image is something that is given at creation, while the likeness of God is something that a person grows into at a later time, during one's lifetime.

To be in the 'image of God' is to have a functional likeness to God, or to have the divine purpose of God (Genesis 5:1-3). Jesus said, "Whoever loses his life for my sake will save it," calling us into our eternal purpose, where Jesus Christ is our icon (Romans 8:29).

The 'image of God' does not mean a physical image of God, since God is beyond time and space. The Bible says that God's essential nature is spirit, not material (John 4:24). The human spirit must reach out to God internally through a spirit of truth and not merely externally. To live in the 'image of God' begins with commitment to God's purpose and ends with living according to that commitment.

Implications of the Image

When a person is not in the 'image of God', there is what is called an 'exile' -- to be separated from God. For example, when we break God's covenant, we are no longer in God's image, and we are exiled or separated from God. Likewise, when Adam and Eve broke their commitment to God's purpose, they were exiled and cut off from a union with God (Genesis 3:22-24).

Exile has two components:

- **To be dislocated:** In exile, a person is not where they should be; not at home in God's image and not in the place God has given to the person.

- **To know who is in charge:** In exile, God is no longer in charge. There is a battle between the kingdom of God and the kingdom of the world.

The Way Forward

To live the creation mandate is to mirror God's creativity by confronting the chaos and bringing order and goodness (Mathew 26:6-10).

Here are some ways to engage in the creation mandate:

- **Mandate to Work**
  Creation takes work (Genesis 2:7); it means taking something like raw material and making something new out of its creation. This can be education, sports, music, agriculture, technology, science, etc. Work gives a person a sense of worth in his or her creativity; it is the creative engagement with the world on behalf of God. This is becoming increasingly challenging in a world in which 'leisure time' is becoming more of a problem.

- **Mandate for Responsibility**
  Creation takes responsibility. Work is part of the responsibility that God laid on human beings, from the very beginning, even before things could go wrong (Genesis 1:28, 2:15). Since creation belongs to God, misusing it is an act of disrespect and irresponsibility. It is easy to avoid taking this responsibility. For example, one way is by despair. What can I do? What will my talents account for in this world? To despair is to diminish oneself. There is hope.

- **Mandate to Rest**
  True rest is not only to stop our labor, but also to understand God has completed our labor to find fulfillment, and rest in it. While work is meaningful, it should not be viewed as the be-all and end-all. Work alone cannot give meaning to one's life. It is a tool or a means to an end. We must find our comfort zone between work and rest. Rest has the power to open our eyes to

the landscape of our whole life. 'Rest should be used for contemplation and to celebrate 'the joy of life' (Isaiah 43:7).

In closing, the significance of the creation mandate is expressed clearly in John Milton's 'Paradise Lost', which he composed when he was completely blind in both eyes.

John Milton dramatizes creation as a progression through the fall, the redemption, and the final victory. Rebellion against God in the book of Genesis is the 'Fall', leading to a corruption of human thinking and moral choices. When humanity 'falls', God puts a plan in action to rescue his creation and restore it to what it was destined to be. Through Jesus' death and resurrection, the fallen condition of the world is redeemed.

The victory that the return of Christ will accomplish in the end is not yet fully visible. Christ will return to fulfill the final victory and reverse the loss of paradise. In the interim, God is shaping a people whose responsibility it is to seek His truth and represent Him.

Why is
Jesus the
Son of God
called
the "Word"?
Is it because
He is the
medium
by which God
communicates
His will and
gives His
commandments?

Chapter 2

Logos Demystified

Logos: the divine wisdom manifest in the creation, government, and redemption of the world

In the secular worldview, Logos is a technical term used for the principle of order and knowledge, which includes the natural law, the moral law, the social law, etc. In Hebrew, Logos is an expression for the divine God. In Greek, Logos is one of the three modes of persuasion and appeal by the speaker or writer to their audience. These include ethos, pathos, and logos. Ethos is an appeal to the authority and credibility of the presenter. Pathos is an appeal to the audience's emotions. Logos is logical appeal used to support the speaker's claims or thesis.

In the Bible, the Gospel of John identifies the Christian Logos, the divine reason through which all things are made, ordering it and giving it form and meaning. Additionally, John identifies Jesus Christ as the Logos in physical bodily form. Logos is active, alive, and comes with divine power because it originates from God. It can be either the written Word as in the Bible, or the spoken Word as in hearing the gospel message.

The Bible explains that Logos is the Word of God and the means by which God accomplishes the acts of creation. For example, when God said, "Let there be light" (Genesis 1:1-4).

John presents Logos as both the "Word of God" and Jesus Christ (John 1:1-5, Revelations 19:13,16). And the Word became flesh, and dwelt among us (John 1:1-4).

Word with an upper-case 'W' indicates divine person. Words are important because they convey thoughts. A 'word' is an expression with which we articulate speech and communicate. The 'Word of God', Logos, then, is 'the divine' expressing in audible terms.

The Son of God is called the "Word" because He is the medium by which God communicates His will and gives His commandments. His name is called "The Word of God" (Revelations 19:13, Hebrews 1:1-3).

Let's suppose that I have many thoughts in my mind and many kinds of emotions in my heart. Unless there was some way to communicate these to others, there is no way for others to know them. Words are a channel by which we convey thoughts to others. The Bible says, we are what we think (Proverbs 23:7). From this perspective, words are also a tool to convey what we are to others.

Why do we need the Logos?
Jesus Christ is called "the Word" because he is the medium by which God communicates His will and gives His commandments. The Word is not reserved for a select group of elite people like clergy, powerful, wealthy, or priests. It is for anyone who puts their faith in Jesus Christ.

"God can be worshipped in the cathedral or in the laboratory. His creation is majestic, awesome, intricate, and beautiful" (Francis Collins, *The Language of God*).

Here are some ways to view the Word of God:

- **The Word is Active**
  It is active and comes with divine power because its source is God (John 1:1).

- **The Word is Eternal**
  Eternal life is to know God (John 17:3); Since God does not have a beginning or ending, His qualities do not have a beginning or an ending – His love, mercy, and justice are eternal.

- **The Word is Purpose**
  The Word gives us meaning and purpose. Every word implies a thought; thoughts imply a resulting action. Thoughts and actions are inseparable (Isaiah 55:8).

- **The Word is Light**
  God is light, light represents truth and is a metaphor for goodness. Darkness is similar to ignorance and error; Satan masquerades as an angel of light (Genesis 3:1).

- **The Word is a Living Hope**
  The abiding of God's Word is equal to God himself abiding in us through the unchanging word of God. The Word is a foundation, it saves, instructs and is our anchor in life (1 Peter 1:23-25).

- **The Word is Life**
  The Word of God is spirit and life to those who believe (John 6:63).

Now what? How do we follow the Logos-Word?

"The Bible is alive, it speaks to me; it has feet, it runs after me; it has hands; it lays hold of me" (Martin Luther, *Treatise on Good Works*). To follow Christ means to have our heart and conscience aligned to the Word of God. To follow Christ is not about hiding behind external norms, and rituals.

Here are some ways to follow the Word:

- **Not by Works, Faith alone**
  We cannot receive the Word of God through our good works, it can only be received by faith. Faith is the conduit to our salvation. Through the Word, we have faith in Christ (Romans 5:1). And since faith can only be experienced in the inward, we believe with the heart (Romans 10:10).

- **Justified and Set Free**
  We are justified through the merits of Christ alone, in whom we place our faith (Romans 1:17). Therefore, we are set free through faith in Christ. Without Christ, we will potentially bring about a spiritual suicide. "Thou hast destroyed thyself; but in me is thine help" (Hosea 13:9).

Unity of the Word and Spirit

To follow Christ means the union of the Word and the Spirit of Christ. The inner feeling or conviction in our spirit and the Word have to be united. Some of us seek the inner conviction without the Word of God. Others seek it in the Word without the leading of the Spirit. (Andrew Murray, *With Christ in the School of Prayer*).

In closing, following the Logos-Word demands discipleship, without which it becomes cheap. To be a disciple of Christ means to have allegiance for Christ and become Christ-like when we strive to follow the Word of God. Dietrich Bonhoeffer compares cheap grace with costly grace, writing:

Cheap grace is the grace we bestow on ourselves. Cheap grace is the preaching of forgiveness without requiring repentance... grace without discipleship, grace without the cross, grace without Jesus Christ, living and incarnate. Costly grace is the gospel which must be sought again and again… "It is costly because it condemns sin, and grace because it justifies the sinner" (Deitrich Bonhoeffer, *The Cost of Discipleship*).

Do you have
a personal
relationship
with God
or is it merely
an intellectual
knowledge
about God?

Chapter 3

Knowing God and Known by God

Knowing: having or reflecting knowledge, information, or intelligence

Knowing is the state of being aware or informed. The English word 'know' is a translation of the Greek word ginosko, which, means personal knowledge, as in experiential knowing. There are different types of knowing. When you truly know God, it is not simply an intellectual understanding of facts about God or theoretical knowledge of the Bible. It is a personal relationship that involves the thinking mind, feeling heart and free will. It is not mechanical. This is an essential aspect of knowing God.

God is known in the soul where thinking, feeling and volition (power of using one's will) occurs. As we submit to God's authority, and regulate all the details of our life by His commandments and rules, we regulate our thoughts and behavior. "Then shall we know, if we follow in the paths of obedience to know the Lord" (Hosea 6:3).

It is not just about what you know; it is about what you do! Without obedience, we will not be able to know God even if we fill our intellect with all kinds of knowledge. Knowing God calls for humility in place of pride. We know God if we keep His commandments (1 John 2:3).

The opposite of knowledge is ignorance. Ignorance is the lack of knowledge. Ignorant people are either unaware or uninformed. The Bible says, "My people are destroyed from lack of knowledge" (Hosea 4:6). One basic strategy that Satan uses is to keep people ignorant (2 Corinthians 4:4).

Knowledge strengthens us spiritually by feeding our faith. In the Bible, the words 'to know' and 'to believe' are used interchangeably. If we know Him, we keep His commandments (1 John 2:3). To know God is to labor for God in our actions. The people who know their God, do great exploits because they are sensitive to God's truth. "The people that do know their God shall be strong, and do great exploits" (Daniel 11:32).

Why people may not want to know God?

For C.S. Lewis, there was simply no good reason to believe in God. Early in life, Lewis was bitter toward religion and felt betrayed by God. He did not want to know God since the suffering he had witnessed and experienced in World War-I; seemed irreconcilable with the existence of a good God. However, the question of God's existence would not let him go.

Both J.R.R. Tolkien and C.S. Lewis had fought in World War-I before returning to Magdalen college. Tolkien helped answer a question that troubled Lewis since childhood: how could every other religion be false and Christianity be true? Lewis realized that he did not need to declare every other religion and myth completely false; they were echoes or anticipations of the total truth, which was known only in and through Christianity.

Lewis would later explain this with an illustration: there is only one right answer to a sum, such as $2 + 2 = 4$, and there are many wrong answers. But some wrong answers are closer to the right answer than others. A few months after this conversation, the final pieces fell into place and Lewis became a Christian.

Why Should we Know God?
C.S. Lewis said, "I believe in Christianity just as I believe that the Sun has risen, not only because I see it, but because by it I see everything else." He could see the Sun, and with that Sun he could see and know everything else around him.

Knowing God is the essence of the Christian life (John 17:3). We are created to know God, which is the highest form of knowledge. If we truly know God, our life will display courage, humility, truth, and other Christian virtues that are a natural by products of 'knowing God.'

Without knowing God, the world becomes a strange and painful place for us to live. Life becomes disappointing; we will stumble and blunder through life. In the end, not knowing God will destroy our body, soul and spirit, just as one leak will destroy and sink a ship. John Bunyan said, "One leak sinks a ship, and one sin will destroy a sinner" (John Bunyan, *Pilgrims Progress*).

How do we know God?
Knowing God is a matter of personal experience with God, and not about theology or reason. Theology is religious beliefs when it is developed systematically. It is the heart which experiences God, and not the reason. This, then, is faith: God felt by the heart, not by the reason. Reasoning helps to arrive at faith, it does not bring one to faith (Blaise Pascal, *Pensees*).

Here are some ways for knowing God:

• **Knowing the Mind and Heart**
  Knowing God is a personal relationship that takes your

thinking mind, feeling heart and free will. This means walking in the ways of God and knowing the mind and heart of God. It is not about knowing facts about God or having the right notions in one's head. We know God through the Word of God in our heart and acting upon it (1 John 2:4)

- **Budgeting time for the Body, Mind and Spirit**
  Since we are created as body, mind and spirit, we need to be well-balanced physically, mentally and spiritually. The physical body, mental body and spiritual body must "grow in the grace and knowledge of the Lord Jesus Christ" (2 Peter 3:18). To grow in grace is to mature as a Christian. The body is the temple of the living God, so we are to care for it. By having a strong connection to the holy spirit inside us, we can experience the spirit of love, joy, and hope instead of hate, fear, and anxiety in our spirit.

- **Developing Spiritual Disciplines**
  Spiritual discipline opens the door for freedom and knowing God. Inward disciplines include meditation, prayer, fasting and study. Outward disciplines include simplicity, solitude, submission and service. Corporate disciplines include confession, worship, guidance and celebration (Richard Foster, *Celebration of Discipline*).

Just as an athlete experiences freedom through physical discipline, a believer in Christ experiences freedom through spiritual discipline. For example, fasting is a spiritual discipline for the body, mind, emotions, and the spirit.

In the end, knowing God means to move out of our comfort zone. For example, William Carey left the comfort of his home in England and came to Calcutta, India in 1793. As a young man, when William accepted Christ, his interests began to expand. When he realized that multitudes of people were perishing without the knowledge of God, he volunteered to be the first missionary to India. Though he faced much hardship in India, including financial bankruptcy, wife's mental illness, death of his children - he persevered in his missionary work and translated the Scriptures into Bengali, Oriya, Marathi, Hindi, Assamese, and Sanskrit and other languages. He wrote: 'Expect great things from God; attempt great things for God.'

Is your
Christian faith
founded on
reconciliation
with God
and with others?
Or are you
alienated
from God?

Chapter 4

Meaning
of the Cross

*Cross: the intersection of two ways or lines; the cross on which Jesus
was crucified*

I n the ancient world, the crucifixion was a symbol of death
and horror. It was the most cruel form of execution – a kind
of delayed death in order to maximize pain and suffering. It
was reserved for slaves, foreigners, and rebellious persons. It
symbolizes death.

In the Christian faith, the cross is the intersection of God's love
and justice, not death. God's justice demands punishment for sin
but God's love wants reconciliation and restoration to save sinners
(John 1:29). Sin and reconciliation meet at the cross.

The Hebrew word for sin ishata. It literally means "to go astray" or
failure to fulfill a goal. While God's laws provide a path to life, sin
involves straying from that path (Mathew 22:37-39). Reconciliation
is the act of getting two things to be compatible with each another.
In Hebrew, the word reconcile is kaphar, which means to cover, to
atone or cancel. In the Christian worldview, reconciliation is the
end of enmity and estrangement between God and humanity. It
begins with reconciliation to God and continues to reconciliation
with others.

Historically, humans have been in a state of alienation from God.

For example, failure of humans to get along with each other is a reflection of alienation from God. Through atonement, humanity is made 'at one' again at the cross (Romans 5:11). The first time the word atonement occurs in the Bible is associated with boat-building. God said to Noah, "The end of all flesh has come before Me; for the earth is filled with violence because of them; and behold, I am about to destroy them with the earth. "Make for yourself an Ark of gopher wood; you shall make the ark with rooms, and shall cover it [w-kaphar'ta] inside and out with pitch" (Genesis 6:13-14).

Covering the ark, inside and outside, was an action that would save the people. Without it, the boat would take in water and sink. Atonement works in the same manner; it covers and solves the problem. Without atonement, we will sink and die without hope.

In Hebrew, atonement is the covering for wrongs. The ark is symbolic of God's salvation. On the cross, Jesus atones for mankind who is alienated from God (1 John 2:2). The atonement symbolizes death and life. Seeking atonement was asking to live! It was asking God to cover us so we could live.

Why is the Cross Relevant?
In the biblical worldview, sin was transferred to the scapegoat. A scapegoat means a person or thing taking the blame for others. At the cross, Jesus became the scapegoat for us, thus cancelling guilt and inviting justice.

Again, when Christ was tempted in the wilderness to bow down to the Devil's offer of the kingdoms of the earth, Jesus refused. There are no genuine kingdoms on this earth – only those pretending to be one, through science, entertainment, pleasures, riches, deception, delusion, etc.

The cross is not just a one-time event in history. It is a daily living and style of bearing one's cross. Isaac Watt's famous hymn, "When I survey the Wondrous Cross" portrays the theme of dying to the world at the cross of Christ:

When I survey the wondrous cross
On which the prince of glory died
My richest gain I count but loss
And pour contempt on all my pride
…
Love so amazing, so divine
Demands my soul, my life, my all

How to apply the Cross to Daily Life?

Just as we reveal our character through our actions, Christ revealed the character of God by going to the cross. We are justified through faith in Jesus Christ (Romans 3:25-26). Here are some ways to apply the cross to daily living:

God's Love

The evidence of God's love is the cross. Even though the cross does not provide an explanation for human suffering, it provides a viewpoint from which to bear it, to live, to serve, and to die. It provides a strong place to stand from which to operate. The cross is not a defeat. Rather, it is a victory that was won and demonstrated through resurrection. Through Christ, the believer can experience what C.S. Lewis calls 'divine love'.

He wrote:
Divine love enables a person to love without any direct personal benefit, while most other forms of love are at some level motivated by a desire to fulfill a self-interest. This unique form of love did not simply evolve from human experience, but rather, was implanted in every human being by God through 'moral law' (C.S. Lewis, *The Four Loves*).

Conquer Evil

Not only did Christ go to the cross to atone for our sins and reveal the character of God, he also died to conquer the powers of evil. The Bible says that we have victory through (1 Corinthians 15:57). Through Christ we will overcome and not be defeated, conquer instead of repress, and overpower instead of subdue. What looked like destruction and defeat (Genesis 3:15) turned into renewal and restoration.

Celebration

Freedom from fear and anxiety forms the basis for celebration. At the cross, Jesus turned our mourning into dancing (Psalm 30), which demonstrates the true notion of greatness. Jesus said, "these things I have spoken to you that my joy may be in you, that your joy may be full (John 15:11). Celebration and singing are a unique aspect of Christian worship because we are forgiven through the cross of Christ. The cross is reason to celebrate because we have been set free (Nehemiah 1:8).

In closing, Charles Simeon was an English evangelical who left an unforgettable impression upon his generation. Here are some of his thoughts on enjoying the cross (Handley Carr Glyn Moule, *Charles Simeon*). He wrote:

At the cross, Christ had done for him what he could not do for himself. Every Christian needs the humility to apply one's mind to one's particular calling in life, and watchful over the evils of the heart.

There are but two lessons for a Christian to learn:

- To enjoy God in everything and
- To enjoy everything in God

Do you
have a
covenant
relationship
with God?
Are you
walking in
His ways,
turning
neither to
the right
nor the left?

Chapter 5

What is a Covenant?

Covenant: a usually formal, solemn, and binding agreement

The word 'covenant' comes from the Latin word con venire, meaning a coming together. It is a formal agreement between two or more persons or parties, where they agree to do or not to do something. Both parties have clear obligations and responsibilities.

To live a life of significance, one must understand the power of a covenant. To have depth and success in anything one does, whether it is a personal relationship or a business transaction, it is important to harness the power of a covenant.

A covenant is not the same as a contract. A contract is a written and binding agreement between two or more, enforced by the law for a limited period of time. It is invalid when it is violated by one of the parties involved. On the other hand, a covenant remains intact even if it is violated or breached by one of the parties.

The purpose of a covenant is to reveal a relationship of commitment between two parties, such as between God and His people (Genesis 17:2, Exodus 24:7) or between people (Genesis 21:27). In a covenant, one member's failure does not destroy the relationship. For example, even in judgment, God pronounces His covenant love to raise up, rebuild, restore, and replant, reflecting His mercy (Amos 9:11-15).

In Hebrew the idiom for initiating a covenant is "to cut a covenant" - made by the shedding of blood. There are two covenants - Old and New. In the Old Covenant, a covenant requires a sprinkling of blood on both parties, the alter and the people. The covenant shows that both God and the people are mutually bound by the covenant. God was bound to the people to support, defend, and save them; the people were bound to God to obey God's Word, to love, and serve Him (Deuteronomy 7:9).

Jesus is the mediator of the New Covenant. Jesus' death on the cross amends for justice on the one hand and reconciles mankind to God on the other (Mathew 26:28). Being a follower of Christ is about commitment to a life that Christ has demonstrated for us, not just intellectual acceptance. This means a commitment to God's truth in all aspects of one's life: in our relationships, belief, behavior, finances, marriage, career, social, and business life.

Why is the Covenant Important?
A covenant is a spiritually binding relationship made between God and His people that includes certain agreements, benefits, conditions, and outcomes. For example, marriage is a covenant (Malachi 2:13-14) which is not simply a means for love and happiness. The Bible views marriage as a covenant union designed by God to increase the capacity of both partners to carry out their divine purpose for advancing God's kingdom (Tony Evans, *Kingdom Man*).

As with any relationship, the condition of the heart is crucial. A covenant is built upon love and faithfulness. In his book *The Two Covenants* Andrew Murray lists the following benefits of a covenant:

- A revelation of His purposes – what God was willing to work in those with whom the covenant was made.

- A divine pattern of the work God intended to do – so that we Know what to desire, expect, etc.

- A security and guarantee of the things that God has promised to bring to pass with those He has entered into a covenant.

- The anchor of the soul – pledging God's authenticity and faithfulness.

- To give mankind a hold upon God, who keeps covenants to link men and women to God, to bring us to make God the portion and the strength of our soul.

How to Practice a Covenant Mindset?

Covenants are foundational in the Bible. In the Old Covenant, the transformation of a person's inner being was accomplished by observing God's laws externally (Deuteronomy 30:6). However, in the New Covenant, the transformation is achieved internally through faith in Jesus Christ. Through His death on the cross, Jesus shed His blood as a sacrifice for the forgiveness of sins, which is the foundation of the New Covenant. This covenant is based not on the external observance of laws and regulations, but on an inner transformation of the heart through faith in Christ.

Human Responsibility

Every command in the Bible is evidence of human responsibility as well as God's sovereignty. God's sovereignty is incomplete without human responsibility. Responsibility brings freedom and helps us to be the person that God destined us to be. In his book Man's Search for Meaning, Viktor Frankl explains that our ability to respond to life and be responsible to life is key to finding meaning and therefore, fulfilment in life. Responsibility is the essence of our existence. He believed that humans were not simply the product of heredity and environment and that they had the ability to make decisions and take responsibility for their own lives (Frankl, *Man's Search for Meaning*).

Roadmap

Covenants are crucial to God's redemptive plan to restore humanity to its divine calling. God's covenant relationship is like a road map with plans, time-line, and milestones. A roadmap shows what is happening in one's life and also how it fits within the big picture of God's covenant relationship with us. All we have to do is stay in tune with God's truth and Word. God's Word is a guide to keep us on track and make progress. God has a good plan for our life (Jeremiah 29:11).

Covenant Blessings

Obedience to God's covenant is not meant to be a burden, but rather a blessing. Blessings are not necessarily about physical wealth or health. The New Covenant is about the inner transformation of the heart through faith in Christ.

In closing, covenant is serious business. It is not only knowing about the covenant, but also the covenant keeping God. Edward Mote sums the meaning of covenant well in his hymn "My Hope is Built on Nothing Less" based on Mathew 7:24-27:

My hope is built on nothing less than Jesus' blood and righteousness; I dare not trust the sweetest frame, but wholly lean on Jesus' name.	When darkness veils his lovely face, I rest on his unchanging grace; in every high and stormy gale, my anchor holds within the veil.
On Christ, the solid Rock, I stand: all other ground is sinking sand; all other ground is sinking sand.	His oath, His covenant, His blood Support me in the whelming flood When all around my soul gives way He then is all my hope and stay.

Do you
refuse to
give up on
yourself
in the face
of adversity?
Do you
have the
ability
to suffer
greatly and
grow from it?

Chapter 6

Resilience

Resilience: an ability to recover from or adjust easily to misfortune or change

Resilience is the ability to bounce back from difficult circumstances. It is our capacity to recover from or overcome difficulties, misfortunes, tragedy, adversity and other sources of hardship.

In physics, resilience is the capacity of an elastic material (such as rubber) to absorb energy (such as from a blow) and release that energy as it springs back to its original shape. The recovery that occurs is comparable to a person's ability to bounce back after a setback.

A good way to picture resilience is through a boxing match between two opponents who go between taking punches (being tough) and getting knocked down (bouncing back). The fighters often rely on their opponent's mistakes in order to gain advantage or to bounce back. When the boxer takes punches, they learn to be tough from the damages. When a boxer is knocked down during a fight, they are expected to return to their feet and defend themselves. It is critical to remain in the fight, even in a beaten form, to avoid failure. If you don't get back up again, it can be viewed as a loss.

Being resilient does not mean being unaffected by the tragedies of life. We have the ability to suffer greatly and grow from it. We show personal resilience when we experience the death of loved ones and other losses. When people refuse to give up on themselves and the world, even after misfortune, they are being resilient.

Though resilience is good, too much resilience can be dangerous when you are overly tolerant of adverse circumstances that are unpleasant or counter-productive. Rather than pushing for change, you will consistently follow goals that are damaging. At work, this can translate into putting up with boring or demoralizing jobs or bosses for longer than needed.

The Bible demonstrates resilience this way:
• When God takes a painful circumstance in our life and not only heals us, but also makes us even stronger than we were before the painful experience.

• When we press on forward (Philippians 3:13-15), overcome hardship and temptations (Romans 12:21), and persevere in the face of trials and suffering (James 1:12).

• When we stand firm in the faith at difficult times (John 17:17).

Why Resilience?
Resilience is not a fixed trait that some people have and others don't. We have the ability to rise up from adversity by thinking and acting in ways to navigate through tough times.

Resilient People have the following qualities:

• Resilient people are willing to accept the situation that they are in and acknowledge that suffering is part of life. Even though they are not welcoming suffering, they accept it as a part of life. Knowing this helps one to say, 'why not me?', as opposed to 'why me?' "Should we accept from God only good and not adversity?" (Job 2:10).

42

- Resilient people choose where to place their attention, energy and focus. They build resilience by taking control of the things that they can change, instead of what they cannot change. They choose to focus on positive things that are within their control. "The Lord makes firm the steps of the one who delights in him; though he may stumble, he will not fall, for the Lord upholds him with his hand" (Psalm 37:23,24).

- Resilient people ask themselves if what they are doing is helping or harming them. They are not afraid to ask, "Is the way I am thinking and acting helping me or harming me?" They learn to be kind to themselves and maintain control over their decision making.

How do I Cultivate Resilience?

How resilient we are will depend heavily on where we focus our energy—inside ourselves or outside of ourselves. If we focus inward on the things we can change, we will adapt well to difficult circumstances and bounce back. We will take personal responsibility for how well life goes. We don't wait for others to rescue us. Through faith, Scripture, prayer, and inner strength, we work through our feelings, set goals, and emerge resilient (Micah 7:8).

A person who believes that their life is under the control of outside forces acts in ways to validate and fulfill that belief. For example, an individual who feels helpless, victimized, and blames others, will live out of beliefs in external control. They do not believe that their personal efforts will make any difference; their happiness depends on other people and forces they cannot change. They don't take responsibility or action when suggestions are offered.

Here are some ways to cultivate resilience:

- **Focus.** Focusing on small, attainable goals; on things you can change.

- **Maintain a Positive Attitude.** Taking the time to laugh, appreciate good moments, and "smell the roses" daily increases one's resiliency.

- **Regulate Emotions.** Taking ownership of your feelings and controlling them.

- **See Failure as Helpful Feedback.** Rather than internalizing failure or blaming, a resilient person looks for lessons in personal failure. They might ask, "What can I do better next time?" or "What can I learn from this?"

- **Have Faith.** Faith leads to resiliency in that it overcomes; it is not a victory that expresses itself in leisure. It rises in adversity. We are to "lay aside every weight, and...run with endurance the race set before us" (Hebrews 12:1).

- **Overcome Fear.** Don't be afraid to ask for help; Fear weakens one's resilience, narrows cognitive functions and limits action choices.

The Bible captures the essence of resilience in this way: "Rejoice not over me, my enemy! Though I have fallen, I will rise. Though I sit in darkness, the Lord will be my light... until he pleads my case and upholds my cause. He will bring me out into the light; the day for building my walls will come, the day for extending my boundaries". (Micah 7:8-11)

Are you
aware that
we are always
under attack
by the enemy?
And that we
overcome
through the
blood of
Jesus Christ
and the
testimony of
the word?

Chapter 7

Know
Your Enemy

*Enemy: one that is antagonistic to another, especially one seeking to
injure, overthrow, confuse, or frustrate an opponent*

The root word for enemy in the Latin is inimicus, meaning
hostile or unfriendly, and comes from the prefix 'in' for'
not,' and 'amicus', for 'friend'. An enemy is not a friend.
An enemy can also be a thing or a spirit that harms or weakens
someone. Other words used to describe an enemy are an adversary,
foe, opponent, rival, and antagonist.

The Hebrew word for adversary is satan, and is derived from a
verb meaning 'to obstruct, oppose'. Some of the emotions
associated with the enemy are anger, hatred, frustration, fear,
threat, and distrust. The Latin word for devil is 'diabbolus,'
meaning 'false accuser and slanderer'.

The Bible teaches us to awaken and recover ourselves from being
taken captive by the traps of the devil (2 Timothy 2:26). The devil
opposes God's presence, purposes, and people in this world
through deception, accusation and lies (1 Chronicles 21:1,
Revelation 12:10; 13:6). Some of the remedies against Satan's
devices are the Word of God, prayer, fasting, and spiritual gifts
(Ephesians 6:10-18).

We overcome the enemy through the blood of Jesus Christ and
the Word (Revelation 12:11). Here are a few distinctions between
God and the devil:

Qualities of God	Qualities of the devil
Uncreated being, eternal	Created being, not eternal
Ultimate purpose is to restore and prosper you via truth and restoration	Ultimate purpose is to destroy you via lies, deception, accusations, and half-truths
Present everywhere, unlimited and infinite	Restricted, limited, finite and subservient to God

Why you should know the enemy?
We are deceived and deluded because we reject or lack knowledge about the enemy (Hosea 4:6).

The devil seeks to steal, kill, and destroy (John 10:10). For example, the devil may try to steal your happiness, fulfillment and ultimately your life by drawing you into addictions and habits that can harm you. However, we have no reason to fear since we have been given the power and resources to fight the enemy.

Knowing our enemies helps us to stay alert, vigilant, and disciplined. For example, God did not create us to live in isolation, which will make us more vulnerable to enemy attacks. When we are ignorant of our enemies, we become complacent, timid, and disengaged. Knowing our enemy helps to anticipate enemy actions before they attack.

If we underestimate the spiritual enemy, we will go to the battle unarmed, and be easily defeated without the right weapons. If we overestimate the enemy, we will lose confidence in the face of evil to stand against the devil's schemes.

How do you fight the enemy?
We can fight the enemy by drawing near to Jesus Christ and His Word: "And they overcame him by the blood of the Lamb and by

the word of their testimony" (Revelation 12:11). To stand against the devil's schemes, the Bible teaches us to put on the full armour of Christ. For example, God's truth, stand against evil, peace, faith, protect the mind, and the Word of God (Ephesians 6:10-18, Isaiah 59:17).

Here are some ways to fight the enemy:

- **Resist the enemy with the Word, do not make treaties**
  Knowledge of the Word of God is essential for resisting the enemy. The Bible teaches us to resist and fight against the devil (James 4:7). It is safe to resist the enemy but not safe to argue, dispute, or make treaties with the enemy (Deuteronomy 7:2). When Satan tempted Jesus after 40 days of fasting, the devil quoted scripture to Jesus. Jesus resisted Satan using Scripture. The devil uses scripture, so it's very important to know the Scripture, memorize it, and meditate on it (Ephesians 6:17).

- **Be willing to think**
  Thinking is important, but it is hard work. It is much easier to have someone else think for us. The Bibles says that we are what we think (Proverbs 23:7). Lacking or rejecting knowledge leads to destruction (Hosea 4:6). We are encouraged to think through the Word of God. This is done intentionally by planting good thoughts from the Word of God so that these thoughts can take root and grow. Eventually, these good thoughts will remove the destructive thoughts that the enemy has planted in your mind.

- **Activate Christ**
  If Christ is activated, then we are armed against the enemy (Romans 13:14). To activate Christ means to appropriate God's power in a personal way in one's daily life. When the enemy

comes, it is natural to fear. Yet, what we do with that fear impacts the outcome. We need a courageous spirit to obey God (Joshua 1:7). The fearful will march for Hell (Revelation 21:8).

In closing, Jesus destroyed the works of the devil by going to the cross and rising again (1 John 3:8). Jesus has authority over the devil (Mathew 4:10, Deuteronomy 6:13). The Protestant Reformer Martin Luther describes this thought elegantly in the hymn he wrote:

"A Mighty Fortress is our God",
taken from Psalm 46.

"A mighty fortress is our God, a bulwark never failing
Our Helper He, amid the flood of mortal ills prevailing
For still our ancient foe doth seek to work us woe

And though this world with devils filled should threaten to undo us
We will not fear, for God hath willed His truth to triumph through us
The Prince of Darkness grim, we tremble not for him

His rage we can endure, for lo, his doom is sure
One little word shall fell him"

~ Martin Luther

Which
kingdom
do you want to
be a Citizen of?
The Kingdom
of God or
the Kingdom
of Satan?
It is up to us
to choose the
way, the truth
and the life that
God offers us.

Chapter 8

The Kingdom
of Heaven

Kingdom: a realm or region in which something is dominant
Heaven: a place or condition of utmost happiness, something that is
very enjoyable
World: the earthly state of human existence

Heaven is simply beyond earth, both in the sense of being physically out of reach and of being higher and greater. In Hebrew, heaven is the dwelling place of God. The word 'heaven' is used interchangeably for 'God'. Out of respect, the Hebrew culture does not pronounce God's name, and instead substitutes God for 'heaven' or 'Almighty One' (Luke 15:21). The opposite of heaven is Sheol or hell, the underworld place of stillness and darkness which lies after death.

In the Bible, hell is described as a place of outer darkness, where there is weeping and gnashing of teeth. Jesus spoke of hell as 'eternal fire', as opposed to Heaven as 'eternal life'. Hades or hell is described as a place of torment or a deep abyss.

The kingdom of Heaven means the reign of God in the world. The world is a place in need of God's saving grace. The kingdom of Heaven has come to the world in the person and mission of Jesus Christ. The kingdom of God is not only concerned with our soul but also with the complete inner transformation of the whole person. The opposite of the kingdom of Heaven is Satan's kingdom where evil reigns. Every choice or action we take moves us closer to God or to Satan.

How do we enter the Kingdom of Heaven?

Entering the kingdom of Heaven is not a physical journey, it is a spiritual journey that is entered through faith and requires personal participation. Rather than an external, mystical or bodily experience either, it is an inward reality that happens by allowing Christ to transform one's heart and mind through faith. The kingdom of God is not forced upon anyone, it must be received willingly with one's free will.

Why is the Kingdom of Heaven significant?

The kingdom of Heaven has significance because it brings deliverance, freedom and salvation to the believer in Christ. In this way, we are brought into God's blessings and delivered from the power of evil. God initiated and established this at creation.

We are created in the 'image of God' to have a functional likeness to God, and to have the divine purpose of God (Genesis 5:1-3). This includes God's command to represent His kingdom on the earth. The Bible says that we are the temple of God and God's spirit dwells within us through Jesus Christ.

Through Jesus, the kingdom of Heaven has entered the world of humans to work in the heart and mind of humans. This happens through inner transformation.

How do we enter the Kingdom of Heaven?

The Bible says that God has entered into the world in the person of Jesus Christ to redeem the world. The kingdom of Heaven is available for all to enter, the choice is ours.

Repentance and Faith: We enter the kingdom of Heaven through faith in Jesus Christ (Mathew 7:13,21). This requires a whole hearted response to believe, repent and turn around to God's ways and truth based on the Word of God. The Hebrew word for repentance is teshuva - 'to return', 'to turn about'.

It is not just a feeling of guilt or remorse. It is a decision to turn away from where we are headed and return to God (Joel 2:12).

Inner Transformation: We enter the kingdom of Heaven through inner transformation which means to change one's way of thinking and acting based on the Word of God. This means to commit to a new path that includes internal transformation of one's heart, mind, thoughts, choices, behavior and actions. For example, to live by God's standards, not the world's standards (Psalm 112: 1).

A good example of inward transformation can be seen in the life of John Newton, an immoral, bitter, angry captain of slave ships. John Newton wrote the hymn 'Amazing Grace':

"Amazing grace! how sweet the sound
That saved a wretch like me!
I once was lost but now am found,
Was blind but now I see."
~ John Newton

Newton had a spiritual conversion during his return voyage to England aboard the ship Greyhound. He awoke to find the ship caught in a severe storm off the coast of Donegal, Ireland, about to sink. In response, Newton began praying for God's mercy, and soon after the storm began to die down. This experience marked the beginning of his conversion to Christianity. He did not radically change his ways all at once; his total reformation was more gradual. He began to read the Bible and view his captives (slaves) differently. Because slave trade was displeasing to God, he repented of it and fought for the abolition of slavery. He was a champion against slave trade with William Wilberforce before the British House of Commons. Just months before Newton's death, the British Parliament made slavery illegal.

We
acknowledge
that there
is evil in the
world and
although we
walk in the ways
of the world,
why do we
expect God's
goodness and
mercy to
follow us.

Chapter 9

To Follow,
To Pursue: Radaph

Follow: to engage in as a calling or way of life, pursue
Pursue: to seek, find or employ measures to obtain or accomplish

In an age of Sports heroes, movie icons and famous figures, who do we follow? Everyone is pursuing something, whether it is a dream, an achievement, or a purpose, and that means everyone is pursuing a "god". The Bible says that God has been pursuing us (Psalm 139:16-17).

In his book, *'Why I am a Christian'*, John Stott talks about Jesus Christ as the 'Hound of Heaven' who pursued me relentlessly even when I was running away from him in order to go my own way. And if it were not for the gracious pursuit of the Hound of Heaven I would today be on the scrapheap of wasted and discarded lives.

Hounds are dogs that have traditionally been used for hunting or tracking because they are excellent at detecting the source of certain scents. The good hound is like a sheepdog that searches for lost sheep. On the other hand, to hound someone is to relentlessly pursue or pester them. In Psalm 23:6, we read, "Surely goodness and mercy shall follow me all the days of my life." God's goodness and mercy does not merely follow us, it will hunt us like a hound.

The Hebrew word for 'follow' is radaph, meaning to pursue, chase and attend closely upon. In Psalm 23, the Psalmist is fully aware of God's goodness following him and does not get away from God's love. He acknowledges that there is evil in the world. Yet he is also able to say that he does not fear evil, because the Lord is with him. He acknowledges that his enemies war against him, but is also able to say that the Lord prepares a 'banquet table' before those very enemies. This awareness teaches him to know that God's goodness and mercy will forever follow him no matter what happens along the way.

At the heart of the Gospel we find that Christ has been in pursuit of us and continues to pursue us. The full display of this relentless pursuit is demonstrated in Jesus Christ becoming human, going to the cross, resurrecting, leaving behind the empty tomb, and giving us abundant life (John 10:10).

Why does God Pursue Us?

God's call to Adam, "Where are you?", is a call to a relationship with God (Genesis 3:23). C.S. Lewis explains that God does pursue us. To make this possible, God instilled within us a desire for Him that would facilitate our response to His pursuit. He shows that man is born with desires that no earthly pleasure can satisfy and that "if I find in myself a desire which no experience in this world can satisfy, the most probable explanation is that I was made for another world."

Here are a few reasons why God pursues us:
- To rescue and restore mankind from the default destiny of spiritual death from straying away from the path (John 3:5).
- To reconcile us in our relationship with Him and each other, which is part of the good news.
- To restore us to His image (Genesis 1:27).

How do we respond to a God who Pursues?

Following Christ gives us the purpose, identity and freedom we have been searching for in the wrong places. We have a choice to make, to follow Jesus Christ who has been pursuing us or go our own way. Here are some suggestions to respond to a God who pursues:

- **Quicken the Spiritual Senses:** We can respond to God by quickening our five spiritual senses of sight, hearing, smell, taste and touch. For example, Augustine of Hippo responded to God to deliver him from the passions of the flesh such as drunkenness and lust (Romans 13:13-14). He wrote: "You have made us for yourself, and our heart is restless until it rests in you."

- **Pursue your destiny:** In the Bible, "destiny" is found in the active sense of fulfilling God's purpose for one's life in one's generation (Acts 13:36). Through faith in Jesus Christ, we can reach our eternal destiny. Next, by the application of God's truth to our life, propelled by faith, we reach our personal destiny (James 2:14). We desperately need Christ; we are not capable of achieving our eternal and personal destiny without God, in whose image we are created for a unique purpose. We must connect with God in our thoughts, attitudes, actions, behavior, and habits. To disconnect with God, is to disconnect with our personal and eternal destiny (Deuteronomy 6:5).

- **Pursue Freedom:** Freedom is foundational in the Bible because we are justified by grace through the redemption that came by Christ Jesus. Christ saved us so we have the freedom to live the way God wants us to live. To be saved means to be free; free from the bondages of the past, and the present, to give us a future, and a hope. We do not earn our freedom through actions or works such as religious rituals, good deeds, or church attendance.

In closing, in his book 'The Confessions', Augustine of Hippo explains that God pursued him to deliver him from the passions of the flesh and lust. He wrote "You made us for yourself and our heart is restless until they find rest in you."

We have
all been
betrayed
at one time
or other
and it can be
devastating.
But is it
possible to
find healing
from its
wounds?

Chapter 10

Betrayal or Allegiance?

Betrayal: violation of a person's trust or confidence, of a moral standard, etc.
Allegiance: devotion or loyalty to a person, group, or cause

Betrayals are devastating, but it is possible to find healing from its effects. We have all been betrayed at one time or other. People will betray us but God will never betray.

The dictionary defines betrayal as the violation of a person's trust or confidence. It disrupts one's life and has emotional consequences such as low self-esteem, anger, bitterness, grief, resentment, and guilt.

Often, betrayal causes one to seek revenge intentionally or unintentionally. Revenge is a form of 'justice' or 'fairness' to restore one's collapsing world. However, it not only destroys the betrayer, but also the person seeking revenge. It is a reality that is created by the mind. However, we can change our reality by changing our mind to the mind of Christ, through God's truth (Isaiah 55:11, John 15:4).

The opposite of betrayal is allegiance, coming from the Latin word alligo, meaning 'to bind'. Allegiance and loyalty are hard to embrace because they require one to think of the other person rather than oneself. They involve responsibility because of the impact on the other person.

In Hebrew, the word allegiance comes from the word shema, which means to maintain loyalty, and dependability. The Jewish Shema Prayer is a daily prayer of allegiance to the God of Israel that excludes allegiance to other gods (Numbers 15: 7-41). It is a command to love God with all of one's heart, soul, and might (Deuteronomy 6:5).

In Genesis 42, when Joseph's brothers bowed to him, he recognized them and remembered the dreams that God gave him foretelling a time when his brothers would bow before him. Even though Joseph had the ability to take revenge on his brothers, he chose to embrace forgiveness because he understood that God's purposes were involved even in 'betrayal'. Because Joseph's allegiance and loyalty were rooted in his relationship with God and God's promises, he was able to move past the betrayals of life. By bringing his emotions to God, Joseph was able to move forward with his life (Proverbs 14:12).

What Causes Betrayal?
Excessive passion, greed, ambition and lust for something can lead to betrayal. For example, the overpowering addiction to wealth, drugs, alcohol or sex. Betrayals are caused by individuals who deceive, and manipulate others for a temporary sense of power.

Why are Betrayals Bad?
We betray ourselves all the time. It takes a lot more effort to show allegiance than betray someone. Betrayal happens where there is trust. The effects of betrayal include disappointment, low self-esteem, loss, grief, shock, anxiety, anger and trauma.

When betrayed, we often seek revenge consciously or unconsciously. The betrayed person's world suddenly collapses, causing grief, sorrow, and depression. Revenge becomes a form of justice. Revenge destroys both the person seeking revenge and the target of the revenge.

Betrayal steals and hijacks one's time and emotional energy. Every time you think of your betrayer, or they dominate your thoughts, they rob your time and energy. This time and energy could have been spent on seeking new opportunities instead of dwelling on the past.

Not only that, you allow the betrayer to be in charge of your life. Being preoccupied with the betrayal or wanting to get even compromises one's quality of life.

How do you stop betrayals from derailing your life?
The bottom line is this: people may betray us but God will never betray us (Job 19:25).

When you feel betrayed, stay focused on God's purpose in that specific situation. Your betrayer is in his or her own prison of misery. Release your betrayer and be free. Jesus was betrayed. Jesus went to the cross so that we can live in freedom. Focusing on revenge interferes with our healing and leads to negative thoughts.

Next, bring your emotions to God. Thinking about revenge interferes with your healing and leads to physical, emotional and mental problems. By bringing our emotions to God, we can move forward with life (Proverbs 14:12). This does not mean that we have to suppress or repress our emotions. Suppressing emotional pain can lead to other physical and emotional pain. Repressing or not expressing emotional pain harmful as well. The Bible teaches us to bring our emotions to God and heal through God's truth. We will know the truth when we seek God (John 8:32).

Finally, God will have the last word, not your betrayer. Though betrayal feels like the end, it doesn't have to be. With God's help and through the Word, you can heal from the betrayal. Forgiveness does not mean excusing the behavior of the betrayer; it means releasing resentment and choosing peace (Job 42:10). And, choosing peace will help us move forward (Exodus 14:15).

We have a choice to make: to move past the betrayals of life or get sucked into them.

A good example of betrayal or allegiance is the life of C.S. Lewis, who felt betrayed by God at a very young age. He was bitter toward religion and did not want to know God since the suffering he had witnessed and experienced in World War I seemed irreconcilable with the existence of a good God. However, his question of God's existence would not let him go. After his conversations with other literary critics including J.R.R. Tolkien at Magdalen college, Lewis became a Christian in 1931. C.S. Lewis wrote :

> The books or the music in which we thought the beauty was located will betray us if we trust to them; it was not in them, it only came through them, and what came through them was longing. These things—the beauty, the memory of our own past—are good images of what we really desire; but if they are mistaken for the thing itself, they turn into dumb idols, breaking the hearts of their worshippers (C.S. Lewis, Mere Christianity).

DISCIPLINES

The disciplines are orderly patterns
of behavior that enable us to think
and work effectively.

Who you are
is not in your
external self.
The real you
is in your
heart and mind;
but how are
you going to
protect
your heart
and mind from
corruption and
enslavement?

Chapter 11

The Battle for the
Heart and Mind!

Battle: to engage in combat between individuals, fight
Heart: one's innermost character, feelings, or inclinations
Mind: embodying mental qualities, intellectual ability

The heart is not merely a physical organ pumping blood to all parts of the body. It is also the 'spiritual chamber' of the body. It is the totality of who we are in the inner life and manifests itself in the outer life.

Just as the integrity of our physical heart is vital to our physical life, in the same way, the integrity of the 'spiritual heart' is vital to our spiritual life (attitude, thoughts, purpose, meaning, destiny) and to physical life (passions, temper, time, work, leisure, finances etc.). In the same way, the brain, intellect, mind is not merely a control center for thoughts, intellect, speech and learning. There is spiritual connection between the heart and the mind.

In Hebrew, lev means 'heart.' However, it is not merely a body part. A person thinks, feels and decides with the heart. It is in the heart that knowing and feeling happen. The spirit (ruah) reflects the heart, including the emotions, attitudes, fear, courage, etc. In the Hebrew, the mind (thought) and heart (understanding) work together. Thoughts and actions are inseparable in the Bible. God will only be perceived by those who seek Him with all their heart (Jeremiah 29:13).

Faith does not oppose reason. Rather, it is above and beyond reason. In his book *'Pensees'* (Thoughts), Blaise Pascal, the French mathematician and Christian apologist writes that we experience God through the heart by grace rather than through reason of the mind. We know truth, not only by the reason, but also by the heart.

Pascal compares the mind to the rational or mathematical mind of pure reason, and the heart to the intuitive mind.

Heart	Filter	Mind
Intuition, realm of feeling. It is our imagination, our experiences, our personality, our deep self. All of these are filters we have which make us see the world differently.	Realm	Pure reason - an aspect of thought which uses premises to arrive at conclusions. Intuition and intellect should be working together.
Discerns the premises. This includes both logical principles as well as ethical principles like doing good and avoiding evil.	Thought	Uses principles and premises to arrive at conclusions. Uses logical reasoning.
Principles are felt by intuition.	Certainty	Propositions are proved
Faith is: God perceived by the heart, not by the reason. Faith is a gift from God, only the heart can receive it.	Faith	Faith is above and beyond reason. Faith does not contradict reason.
We know truth, not only by the reason, but also by the heart. The heart is the basis for truth.	Truth	We know the truth by the reason. Reason is not the basis for truth.

Why are the Heart and Mind Significant?

We are created with a spirit, soul, and body. The spirit is the highest part of us and gives inspiration and understanding (Job 32:8). The body is the 'physical' nature which gives us the five senses. The heart and mind make up the 'soul' nature, which stand as a medium between the spirit and the body (1 Thessalonians 5:23).

The essential nature of God is spirit. Through the spirit, we can connect with God. God is only to be approached in the 'spirit' part of our being (John 6:63, 4:24). Our gifts to God are gifts of the Spirit such as love, purity, boldness, courage, wisdom, faith, generosity, and discernment.

The soul is the 'intermediary' or the 'vessel' through which we communicate with the spirit and body. As the 'vessel', the soul is the container that feeds good and bad things to the body and the spirit. Below is a basic break down of the spirt, soul and body:

Spirit	The human spirit is the innermost and deepest part of a person. Through the spirit, we can connect with God.
Soul	The human soul is the vessel or container through which we think, reason, and experience emotions. It is who we are, our psyche and our personality.
Body	The human body is the visible, external part of our being with five physical senses.

The Way Ahead: Mind to the Heart

The challenge is: How do we go from knowing God in our 'head' to knowing God in our 'heart'? Here are some things to consider:

71

Be Controlled by the Spirit

God's design is that the spirit should rule the heart-mind (John 6:63). In the natural state, the spirit is subservient to the heart-mind, which has earthly passions. In the carnal state, the flesh or body rules the heart-mind. In the spiritual state, the spirit rules the heart-mind.Faith in Christ is made possible by reason of the mind, and emotions of the heart. The Bible calls a life that is based on faith in Jesus Christ as a born-again experience (John 3:3).

Reflection

The Bible teaches us to reflect on our ways by testing and probing our ways (Haggai 1:5). We do this by reflecting inward on a right state of the heart and mind. Reflecting on God's Word will lead to an inner reality that produces good fruits such as love, joy, peace instead of bad fruits of anger, fear, sadness, or bitterness. For example, if we meditate on bitterness, we will begin to burn in anger. If we meditate on God's truth and laws, we will take action to put away the bitterness and anger (Job 11:14). We can reflect based on Philippians 4:8:

- What is true and honorable?
- What is right?
- What is pure and wholesome?
- What is worthy of thought?
- What is lovely?
- What is admirable?
- What is of good reputation?
- What is excellent?

Transform the Mind

How we internalize the Word will determine if the seeds of God's Word fall on good soil, rocky soil, or thorny bushes (Mathew 13: 3-9). The 'soil' is the heart and mind that receives God's truth through the Word of God. The rocky soil describes a heart-mind that is filled with passions of the flesh. The thorny bushes describe soil that chokes the seeds from financial, relational, and family problems. To plant good seeds into good soil, one has to transform the mind (Romans 12:1-2).

In closing, We know truth, not only by the reason, but also by the heart.., We know that we do not dream, and however impossible it is for us to prove it by reason, this inability demonstrates only the weakness of our reason, but not, as they affirm, the uncertainty of all our knowledge. For the knowledge of first principles, as space, time, motion, number, is as sure as any of those which we get from reasoning. And reason must trust these intuitions of the heart, (Blaise Pascal, *Pensees*).

Do you have
baggage from
your past?
Instead of
looking back
in regret
at your past,
are you
willing to do
something
to make your
life better?

Chapter 12

Retrospection

Retrospection: a usually critical look at a past event; the action of looking back on or reviewing past events or situations, especially those in one's own life

Retrospection generally means to look back and reflect on a situation or event. This involves recollecting what went well and identify opportunities for improvement in the future. The Latin source of the word is retrospicere, meaning 'to look back at'. It is like looking in the rear-view mirror. The purpose of retrospection is to get better, be more effective, and to improve on what was learned.

Retrospecting is not about getting stuck on the past or looking back in regret about the past. It is to recollect, to learn from it, and improve the future. For example, some of the questions to ask in retrospection are:

• What worked well?
• What did not work well?
• What are we going to try to do differently?

Retrospection is different from introspection, which refers to looking inward to examine one's thoughts or feelings. Retrospection is about recollecting and contemplating things that happened in the past. Retrospection is not the same as hindsight either: while retrospection is process focused, hindsight is result focused.

Hindsight is the ability to realize the meaning or importance of an event only after it has happened.

To retrospect is to remember

In Hebrew, to remember is zakar, which is not only to recollect the past but to act upon it in the present. In the modern world, time is seen as linear where the past is behind us, and the future is ahead of us, waiting to be explored. However, in the Hebrew Biblical worldview, time is seen from a perspective of observance: the past is in front of us, to learn and grow from, and the future is behind us, unexplored.

It is easy to forget God

When the Israelites remember the Passover, representing the escape from slavery in Egypt, they are instructed to remember the reason they came out of slavery. Moses addressed the Israelites and narrated that God brought them out of slavery. Moses said, "and God brought us out from there, that he might bring us in" (Deuteronomy 6:23). The "bringing out" signifies deliverance or freedom from bondage.

God does not want us to serve Him in bondage. He took them out of the bondage first. This is a clear and resounding message in the Bible. We cannot serve God effectively in bondage of any kind. "That we being delivered out of the hand of our enemies might serve him without fear" (Luke 1:74).

Why are Retrospections Important?

One of the fundamental reasons to do a retrospect is to learn from the past and avoid repeating the mistakes in the future. Retrospection helps us to see everything differently. When Romans 8:28 says, "we know that for those who love God all things work together for good," it means that one day, we will look back in retrospect and see life very differently.

Retrospection helps us to give serious and careful thought to the events of our time. For example, digital addiction has created a harmful dependence on digital media and devices that interferes with retrospective activities like school, work, and sleep.

Retrospection helps us to defend what is good, remove what is harmful, and stay committed to recovery. Retrospection includes a critical look at both the good and bad. To retrospect is to highlight both the successes and failures of an event, and identify areas to improve.

How do we Cultivate Retrospection?

One of the great challenges we face today is finding time for retrospection. We carry our phones and electronic devices with us wherever we go, which are continuously calling for our attention via text messages, digital media, and phone calls. There seems to be no room in our busy schedules to sit quietly, think, and reflect on the information that is made available to us.

Here are some ways to retrospect:

- **Retrospect the past by taking action, don't become captive to it**
  To remember is to act, not merely to bring back to mind. To forget is not to act. One of the best ways to worship is to remember what God has done. 'I will remember the works of the Lord; Yes, I will wholeheartedly remember Your wonders of old' (Psalm 77:11). We have a built-in capacity to forget and many of us default to discouragement. Instead of focusing on how you have messed up, draw your attention to what God has done for you.

- **Remember and Reflect**
  To remember is to bring back to mind while reflection enables

us to see things from God's perspective. God has given each one of us a dream to move forward, to journey on to other places.

In Psalm 20:7 we read: "Some trust in chariots, and some in horses: but we will remember the name of the LORD our God." In the Old Testament, Joseph was a foreign slave and it was next to impossible for Joseph to be freed from a charge of wrong doing. However, the Bible says that Joseph remembered the dream that God gave him in the past. It was a promise from God. He decided to live out that promise and move forward than wallow in self-pity.

Move Forward

We all know what it is like to experience some great difficulty because we knew that there would be joy at the other end. For example, you can take violin lessons and practice your notes over and over until you learn to play the violin. The end goal of long, demanding, and tiring practice is the joy of being able to play something beautiful. Jesus modelled this concept by dying on the cross because he knew that there would be joy at the other end (Hebrews 12:2).

In the end, retrospection and reflection bring us to see past events from God's perspective. God will only be perceived by those who seek Him with all their heart (Jeremiah 29:13).

Did you
know taking
responsibility
is like making a
covenant with
oneself ?
And that
it has the
power to
make life truly
transforming?

Chapter 13

The Power of Responsibility

Responsibility: the quality of being dependable, moral, legal, or mental accountability

Response: something spoken, written, or done in return or reaction to a person or thing that serves as a stimulus

Responsibility comes from the Latin responsus, which means 'to respond.' It holds a sense of responsibility. Taking responsibility is transformative and creates a legacy. It is like making a covenant with oneself.

The word responsibility - 'response-ability'— is the ability to choose your response. Proactive people take responsibility for their response, often looking for what they can learn from what happened. The reactive person complains about how bad the other person is. People who are proactive do not blame circumstances, or conditions for their behavior. Their behavior is a product of their own conscious choice, based on values, rather than a product of their conditions, or based on feeling (Stephen Covey, *The 7 Habits of Highly Successful People*).

The opposite of responsibility is irresponsibility, which shows that you are not thinking enough about possible results or just don't care. We may tell ourselves that we are not to blame, it is someone else's fault, directly or indirectly. We blame the consequences of our personal choices on God, our environment, government, family, or other people.

The Hebrew word for responsibility is achrayut, which is about responding or answering for our decisions and actions. Achrayut comes from the Hebrew word 'acher,' meaning 'other'. It is not just to answer for our own actions but also about our moral commitment to the other person, to make the other's needs our own.

The Bible emphasizes that a person who is responsible in little things, will be faithful in much, and so much is given to that person. In Luke 19 Jesus spoke of a parable where a master gives a 'mina', which is approximately three years' worth of wages to ten of his servants. The master instructed them to 'put this money to work.' We are to take responsibility to 'put our live to work.' An individual who is faithful with the resources that are given such as gifts, talents, treasures, skills, and abilities will be rewarded with greater responsibility. An individual who does not take responsibility will suffer loss with responsibilities and rewards (1 Corinthians 3:12-15).

Why does Responsibility Matter?

When we don't take responsibility for our actions, we tend to blame someone or something else. In Genesis 3, God said, "Adam, what have you done?" "Oh, the woman that You gave me to be my wife, she did tempt me and I did eat." Rather than accept the responsibility for what we have done, we like to throw it over to someone else.

If someone else or something else is really to blame for our mistakes, then we can easily dismiss personal responsibility. If a person is not truly responsible, they are under no obligation to apologize or repent. Without repentance, there can be no forgiveness. Without forgiveness, we will be stuck and our life will not 'take-off.'

The Bible says that we are ultimately responsible to God, since we are created in God's image for good works (Ephesians 2:10). Taking responsibility for our actions will enhance our walk with God, and will improve our relationship with others too.

How do we Take Responsibility?

Responsibility gives us eternal meaning and significance by sharing in God's plan. Here are some ways to take responsibility:

- **Expect great things**

  William Carey pointed out: Expect great things, and Attempt great things. The sovereign God has given each one of us personal responsibility. We are accountable to him for our response to his word, and for the spread of the Word. Therefore we should attempt great things for God. But the reason we attempt great things for God is because we expect our great and our sovereign God to work. Carey had great zeal for God's sovereignty and human responsibility. The 'expecting' and the 'attempting' were 'from God.' (Timothy George, *Faithful witness: the life and mission of William Carey*)

- **Freedom**

  The Bible requires us to take responsibility for our personal freedom (Zechariah 12:2). A clear message throughout the Bible is that we cannot serve God effectively in bondage of any kind (Luke 1:74). In Deut. 6:23, Moses addressed the Israelites and recounted what the Lord had done for them, "and He brought us out of Egypt, that he might bring us into the promised land". The "bringing out" signifies deliverance or freedom from bondage. He did not tell His people to serve Him in bondage. He took them out of the bondage first. We must take responsibility to overcome bondages in our life.

- **Law of Sowing and Reaping**

  Taking responsibility is closely connected to the law of sowing and reaping (Galatians 6:7-8). Sowing is used as a metaphor for our actions and reaping for the outcome of those actions. Wherever we go, we are sowing good seeds or bad seeds in everything we do. Sowing seeds takes responsibility. A tiny seed can produce delicate and beautiful flowers or tough and sturdy trees.

Taking responsibility has a lot to do with who we are and who we are becoming (Romans 12:1-2).

C.S. Lewis puts this in perspective:
"The more we get what we now call 'ourselves' out of the way and let Him take us over, the more truly ourselves we become. The more I resist Him and try to live on my own, the more I become dominated by my own heredity and upbringing and surroundings and natural desire. It is when I turn to Christ, when I give myself up to His Personality, that I first begin to have a real personality of my own" (C.S. Lewis, *Mere Christianity*).

Did you
know that our
perception and
our reality need
not be one
and the same?
We create our
own reality
based on our
perception
and tend to
believe what
we perceive
as truth.

Chapter 14

Change your Perception, Change your Life

Perception: the knowledge gained from the process of coming to know or understand something

The word Perception comes from the Latin word, "percipio" meaning "receiving, collecting, action of taking possession with the mind or senses". Through perception, we experience the world around us and interact with it in ways that are both appropriate and meaningful. Perception is a lens through which we view people, events, and things.

The opposite of being perceptive is to be foolish, unwise, careless and lacking in perception; it is not so much a lack of intelligence as much as it is mental laziness and carelessness. It describes a person who can think but fails to use their power of perception. It is similar to someone who is lacking in discernment.

When we perceive something physically, we receive external information through the physical senses - eyes (vision), ears (hearing), nose (smell), tongue (taste) and skin (touch). This information passes from our physical senses to the mind. When we perceive something spiritually, truth is revealed by the Spirit of God into the human heart and then passes to the mind (Ephesians 4:23). In physical perception, we perceive from the external to the internal, whereas in spiritual perception we perceive from the internal to the external. One passes from the outside to inside, whereas the other passes from inside to outside.

Our perception dictates how we live by creating our own reality. We believe what we perceive to be accurate and then create our own reality based on those perception.

"What you see and what you hear depends a great deal on where you are standing. It also depends on what sort of person you are" (C.S. Lewis, *The Magician's Nephew*). Our experience of life is directly affected by how we perceive.

Why do we need Perception?
When we lack perspective, small things appear to be much larger and more intimidating. Stress builds. We lose our perception. Here are some reasons why perception is important:

- Without proper perception, we will be slow to understand the events and things in our life. Jesus rebuked the disciples for not perceiving the true significance of the miracles.
- Without proper perception, we will be unable to discern. The ability "to see" behind the outward show. It is there to lead us, guide us, help us, warn us, and protect us. We need the Spirit of God to perceive the things of God.
- Changed perception can turn-around events in our life. It can warn us of danger and to take corrective action. For example, Eve was unable to perceive the evil behind the serpent's interpretation.
- When we lack the proper perspective, our life will suffer. With the proper perspective, we can know who we are, whose we are, and why we are in this world.
- Knowing God takes perception. Unless our perceptions change, we can easily become desensitized to the things of God.

How do we Cultivate Spiritual Perception?

The greatest obstacle to spiritual perception is ignorance and lack of knowledge (Hosea 4:6). Here are some pointers for spiritual perception.

- **Meditating on the Word of God:** We are free to choose our own thoughts and perception by meditating daily on the Word of God (Acts 17:11). The Word of God renews our mind and changes our way of thinking and perceiving. For example, we read in the Old Testament that the Israelites were facing a giant name Goliath. The physical perception among the armies of Israel was paralyzing fear and defeat. When David came and evaluated Goliath in a faith-oriented way, it led to a spiritual perception of strength and confidence.

  The same circumstance caused two different kinds of response based on spiritual perception from David and the Israelite forces. The Israelite forces believed they would fail. David believed in God's power and applied a faith-based mindset (1 Samuel 17:37). A mindset is a set of attitudes concerning truth, values, outlook, and disposition. It arises from a person's worldview or beliefs. The faith mindset is built on God's truth and the Word of God.

- **Exercising the Spiritual Senses:** The five senses enable the mind to receive information, emotion process it, reason to judge it for truth, conscience to discern the right and wrong, memory to reject or store it, and finally for hope to see the future. To develop spiritual perception, these senses can be cultivated and exercised.

  We are created with a spirit, soul, and body. The spirit is the highest part of us and gives inspiration and understanding

(Job 32:8). Through the spirit, we can connect with God, whose essential nature is Spirit. God is only to be approached in the 'spirit' part of our being (John 6:63, 4:24). Our gifts to God are gifts of the Spirit such as love, purity, boldness, courage, wisdom, faith, generosity, and discernment.

• **Knowing our enemy:** The best defense against our enemy, the devil, is not only the Word of God and the spiritual discernment, but also to know who are enemy. This includes the strategies that the enemy uses to defeat us (1 Peter 5:8). We resist the devil by standing firm in the faith through Jesus Christ and the Word of God (1 John 5:4, Revelation 12:11). The enemy uses many strategies to divert the believer. In his book '*Paved with Good Intentions*', C. S. Lewis lists how the enemy distracts the believer through diversions, emotional bondages, anxiety, fear, hatred, cowardice, sexuality immorality, not taking time for silence, gluttony, and self-delusion.

A good example of developing spiritual perception through the study of God's Word is captured in the life of the German theologian Martin Luther, who brought about the Protestant Reformation. Luther had become obsessed with Romans 1:17 'The righteous shall live by faith.' Originally, Luther understood the righteousness of God to mean a God who avenges justice by punishing sinners. He admitted that he was angry with God.

Finally, after days of thinking, and meditating day and night, he was able to spiritual perceive the meaning of the verse, He who through faith is righteous shall live. Our righteousness comes through faith in Christ, as it is written: The righteous will live by faith. The whole Bible suddenly took on a new aspect. (Boehmer, Heinrich, *Martin Luther: Road to Reformation*)

Do you
think prayer
is chanting
or a repetition
of scripted
words?
Or is it
reserved for
spiritual
giants, priests,
clergy and
pastors?

Chapter 15

Prayer:
A Discipline

Prayer: to make an earnest request
Commune: to relate and form a close personal relationship

P rayer is like physical exercise; it takes practice and discipline. The more we do it, the more natural it becomes. The English word 'prayer' comes from the old French prier, meaning prayer, petition, or request, and from Latin precaria, which means to 'petition'. The Hebrew verb lehitpallel to pray means 'self-evaluation' and 'to judge oneself.' Prayer shows us our need of God and helps us to enter the presence of God. In praying, one must search the heart and align with God. In prayer, God makes Himself available to us.

Prayer is our way of communing with God. To commune is to communicate intimately. It is a bonding or intimacy between the human (the person seeking or asking) with the divine God (the one who is petitioned or sought). Communing with God can be life changing in that God begins to reveal the secret things and sets us free.

Communing with God is not the same as communication. We can communicate without communing. Communication is the act of exchanging information. Communion occurs when we have a close relationship with Christ. The French mathematician Blaise Pascal wrote, "God instituted prayer in order to give his creatures the dignity of causality."

This means that God wants us to be a part of His creative acts. Prayer allows us to have 'a hand' in what happens. God can only achieve what we request.

Christian prayer is not merely chants or repetitions, nor is it reserved for the spiritual giants, priests, clergy and pastors. Christian prayer is available for anyone to reach out and commune with God freely and spontaneously. Without faith in Christ, a person is spiritually 'dead.' Faith in Christ restores the person who is spiritually dead to become spiritually alive (2 Corinthians 4:16).

How does the human spirit commune with God's spirit?
God's essential nature is Spirit; God is only to be approached in the 'spirit' part of our being (John 6:63). The Bible says that God is spirit, and we are to worship Him in spirit and in truth (John 4:24). In prayer, the human spirit has the ability to connect with God's spirit based on God's truth.

We are created with a spirit, soul, and body. The spirit is the highest part of us and gives inspiration and understanding (Job 32:8). Even after the physical body has died, the spirit will continue to live. Our gifts to God are gifts of the spirit, such as love, purity, boldness, courage, wisdom, faith, generosity, and discernment.

- The human spirit is the innermost and deepest part of a person. Through the spirit, we can connect with God.
- The human soul is who we are, our personality. It is a vessel or container through which we can think, reason, and experience emotions.
- The human body is the visible, external part of our being with the five physical senses.

More Prayer, More Boldness!
Prayer is a way of 'plugging in' to God's power. More prayer leads to more power. If we neglect prayer, the enemy will besiege us.

We read in the Old Testament that the Israelites faced a giant named Goliath, who kept the people of Israel in paralyzing fear. The Israelite forces believed they would fail. David came along and evaluated Goliath in a faith-oriented way that led to feelings of boldness and confidence. David's boldness was based on faith in God's power (1 Samuel 17:37). Prayer brings boldness.

More Prayer, More Power!
The key to prayer and power belongs to God. In Mark 9:25, Jesus rebuked the demon out of the boy: "you dumb and deaf spirit, I command you, come out of him, and never enter him again". This was possible because prayer was a way of life for Jesus. His days and nights were lived in prayer. He was prepared to meet evil when it came. If we neglect prayer, the enemy will prey on us.

How Do We Pray?
Prayer isn't about sending up some words to God. It involves knowing God, listening to Him, and aligning your heart with His. When we are properly aligned, our prayers will get answered. Prayer becomes a conversation. We rarely leverage the power of prayer, and, as a result, are not living out the fullness of our destiny" (Tony Evans, *Kingdom Man*).

Here are some ways to pray:

- **Pray in a Quiet Place:** The Bible teaches us to approach God in the inner chamber of a quiet and secret place. This means that when we approach God in prayer, we are not to be preoccupied with our own thoughts and emotions. Instead, we must withdraw from all that is of the world and prepare to meet God alone. That is, shut out the world and release our self to the secret of God's presence; then, Christ will reveal himself and answer prayer.

- **Pray with God's Word:** The words of our mouth reveal who we are. God reveals himself in His promises, binding himself to those who receive His promises. Praying through God's word enables us to stand firm through the trials and challenges of life. Without prayer and God's truth, we are easily defeated. As we pray, God works. When we run out of words, we can pray using God's Word.

- **Pray with Boldness:** One of the greatest obstacles to praying is that we are often unsure on whether what we ask in prayer is according to the will of God. Without knowing the will of God, we cannot have the boldness to ask in prayer. God's will can be known through the revealed Word of God and spiritual discernment.

In closing, Andrew Murray captures how to pray according to the will of God. He wrote:

"Some seek the will of God in an inner feeling or conviction, and would have the Spirit lead them without the word. Others seek God's will in the word, without the living leading of the Holy Spirit. The two must be united: In the heart, the word and Spirit must meet. Heart and life must day by day be under its influence." (Andrew Murray, *With Christ in The School of Prayer*)

Did you know that biblical meditation is about filling one's mind with the truth of God's word and not emptying the mind?

Chapter 16

Meditation:
A Discipline

Meditation: to focus one's thoughts on, reflect on or ponder over

The word meditation is derived from two Latin words: meditari, which means to think and dwell upon, and medri, which means to heal. The Hebrew word for meditation is hagad, which means active and intense thinking which demands expression.

Secular forms of meditation emphasize the need to become detached from the world and empty our mind of all thought. They emphasize various physical and breathing postures to clear our mind for relaxation or relieving stress.

Biblical meditation is about filling our mind with the truth of God's Word without emptying the mind. Jesus said of the man who had been emptied of evil but not filled with good: "When the unclean spirit has gone out of a person, it is seeking rest and does not find it. Then it goes and brings seven other spirits more evil, and they go in and live there. And the final condition of that person is worse than the first" (Matthew 12:43-45).

By meditating on the Word of God, we are able to bring the mind in harmony with the spirit. The 'mind of the flesh' is controlled by disorder and conflict, whereas the 'mind of the spirit' is governed by life and peace (Romans 8:6). In this way, meditating on God's truth becomes a part of our thinking and feeling.

Meditation is a discipline. When we fix our thoughts on some part of Scripture and meditate, the truth enters our mind and heart. The truth of the meditation becomes a part of our thinking and feeling throughout the day. Much more than noise or silence, meditation involves control. God will take control and strengthen the inner soul.

Why must we Meditate?

Meditation is a way of life. When we meditate, we must go to the presence of God by ourselves without a spokesperson. A spokesperson is someone who is chosen to speak on behalf of others. Jesus went by Himself into the mountainside to pray (Matthew 14:23). A good practice is to go into a solitary and quiet place to meditate.

The purpose of meditation is to be alone with God in our thoughts and feelings. It is not as much about our outer life, as it is about our inner life. We can meditate wherever we are, whether it is working in the office, housekeeping, walking or running. Regardless of where it is done, the aim of meditation is to focus the attention of the body, emotions, the mind and the spirit upon God.

Meditating produces insights that are deeply practical. New perspectives emerge and we are able to successfully navigate through the events of life. For example, when we don't know what to do, God's wisdom is made known to us in meditation. During meditation, instructions come to us on how to deal with a specific situation, problem or opportunity.

Meditating on the truth in God's Word transforms our inner disposition to remain stable even when our external circumstances change. We are able to leave the cares and distractions of the world.

When we memorize scripture and meditate, not only do we keep our thoughts in order, we can also recall it when we need it. The Word stored in memory is a place of rest for the soul, where we become partakers of God's divine nature (2 Peter 1:4).

How do we Meditate?
Meditating on the scriptures is fundamental to faith in Christ. Here are some simple methods to meditate:

- **Read and Memorize God's Word:** Meditation is grounded on Scripture. Reading brings a truth into the mind, while meditation brings it into the heart. For example, during meditation we can focus on different words in the Scripture, and apply it to our daily living for teaching and correction (2 Timothy 3:16). Meditating on God's Word resets the direction of our life, and trains us for good living. During meditation, instructions will come on what to do, what not to do, how to deal with a specific situation, or how to navigate your personal life.

- **Live It Out:** After we prayerfully read God's Word, we meditate on its truth to bring it into the heart. Not only do we meditate on God's Word, we also take action to boldly walk in God's laws (Deuteronomy 28:9). Without bold action, we have the knowledge but fail to put it into practice. For example, Joshua meditated on God's laws day and night before he took bold action to lead Israel into the promised land.

- **Reflect:** We examine God's Word by taking time to reflect over the Scriptures. Reflecting shows the significance of what we are meditating. Reflecting on God's Word will lead to an inner reality that produces good fruits such as love, joy, peace instead of bad fruits of anger, fear, sadness, or bitterness. For example, if we meditate on bitterness, we will begin to burn in anger. If we meditate on God's truth and laws, we will take action to put away the bitterness and anger (Job 11:14).

We can ask several questions based on Philippians 4:8:

- What is true and honorable?
- What is right?
- What is pure and wholesome?
- What is worthy about the content?
- What is lovely in the text?
- What is admirable?
- What is of good reputation?
- What is excellent in the text?

In closing, Thomas Watson states,

"Meditation and practice are like a pair of compasses; the one part of the compass is fixed upon the center, and the other part goes round the circumference: a Christian by meditation is fixed upon God as the center, and by practice goes round the circumference of the commandments".
(Thomas J. Watson, *A Christian on the Mount*)

How do we
die to what
once held us
captive?
How can
we rise above
our past
hurts, habits,
weaknesses,
and become a
liberated person?

Chapter 17

The Power of New Affections

Affection: a feeling of liking and caring for someone or something

H ave you ever struggled to deal with negativity in your life? Have you ever been overcome by personal defects slowing down your progress? Or have you tried to overcome negative habits?

The power of new affections shows that we cannot truly deal with the negative unless we are emphasizing the positive at the same time. To get rid of defects we must cultivate virtues; that is, behavior that shows high moral standards: doing what is right and avoiding what is wrong.

A word that adequately describes this is called 'displacement', to move something from its place or position and filling of the place once occupied by something else. It is the redirection of an emotion or impulse from its original object such as a person, idea or pain. Spiritually speaking, a negative affection is moved from its place of enthronement on our hearts (Romans 6:12). The positive affection that dethrones the negative affection will then arise to the throne and exercise control of one's mind, emotions and will from there (Thomas Chalmers).

The Bible says that faith produces a new affection in exchange for the old affection (1 John 5:4-5). Old affections include the things outside of God that held as captive. This can include our past hurts, being self-centered, old ways of thinking and acting. The new affection is the love of God. New affections are new ways of thinking and acting based on the love of God. The new affection pushes out of our heart the old affection, which is the love of the world. The love of God gives us a new heart, new perspectives, new desires and new potential.

Old affections are our former way of life or 'old self,' which was corrupt and deceitful in its desires. The 'new self' in Christ is completely different. The affections of the 'new self,' is renewed by the transformation of the mind and heart. The old affection is natural, we were born with, and the new affection is supernatural, a gift from God. The old nature cannot please God and the new nature cannot displease God.

Why are Affections Important?
J. I. Packer writes, "We are all, of course, creatures of desire; God made us so, to aim at the extinction of desire is really inhuman in thrust. But desire that is sinfully disordered needs redirecting, so that we stop coveting others' goods and long instead for their good, and God's glory with and through it. New affections seek instead to put God first, others second, and self-gratification last (Ephesians 4:23, 24).

New affections are like the vision of truth that displaces our affection for the shallow things. We cannot simply erase the shallow things in our life. Instead, we must replace them with deep things of God (1 Corinthians 2:10). One taste may give way to another and lose its power entirely as the primary affection of the mind and heart. The Bible teaches us to put on the new self and put off the old self (Ephesians 4:22).

New affections put God first. By our nature, it is difficult and ineffective for the heart to simply withdraw affection. When a new love enters our heart, it can drive out old and stagnant feelings, even attraction for things that was once very attractive.

How do we experience the Power of New Affection?

In the Beatitudes, Jesus shows the new affections of a person who will enter the spiritual world (Luke 6). Just as the secular world produces the character suited to thrive -- self-centeredness, aggression, materialism – the spiritual world too will produce persons of a different character altogether – humility, forgiveness, faith, peace, love, and courage.

Here are some ways to experience the power of new affections:

- **Accentuate the Positive**
  We need to accentuate the positive to eliminate the negative and not mess with the in-between (Colossians 3:1-5). To get rid of the defects is to cultivate the virtues. Instead of withdrawing our affections from an object that is not worthy of attachment, we can set our affections on another object, such as serving God, as more worthy of attachment. It is not simply a question of trying to empty our heart of old affections that are not worthy – quite impossible to do this(John 17:17).

- **Seek the Kingdom of God**
  Through Jesus, the kingdom of Heaven has entered the world of humans to work in the heart and mind of humans. The entry of the Kingdom of God within us happens through inner transformation. Jesus said, "Seek first the kingdom of God … and all these things will be added to you" (Matthew 6:33). Healing begins when we refocus our life on Jesus Christ. Nothing worldly can cure our affections; only an infusion of the supernatural power of Christ can make a lasting difference.

- **Be God-Centered, not Self-Centered**
  Apart from God there is no transformation in the life of a believer. This is the essence of God's love. To experience the power of new affection, we become God-centered and move away from being self-centered. Being God-centered means to stay fixated on God's kingdom in desires, personal relationships and attitudes. Being God-centered means staying committed to God's purpose.

In closing, the essence of the power of new affections is that we have died to what once held us, so that we can be a new person, with new affections, and new perspectives not under the written code of "thou shall" or "thou shall not," but under the code of the spirit (Ezekiel 36:26).

"I feel good,
I like it.
I want it now.
I want more.
Repeat."
Do you
have this
kind of an
uncontrollable
compulsion
to want
something
or the urge to
do something?

Chapter 18

Addictions: Idols of the Heart

Addiction: a strong inclination to do, use, or indulge in something repeatedly

Addictions are everywhere because today's digital culture encourages self-indulgence and excess. Addiction starts off like planting a seed in word or thought, and over time, by nurturing and caring for the seed, it bears fruit.

A Cycle of Addiction works like this:

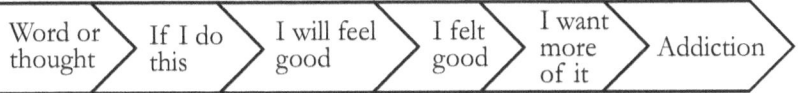

Word or thought > If I do this > I will feel good > I felt good > I want more of it > Addiction

The nature of addiction is such that it fills our life with disorder of every sort: desperation, selfish living, stealing, compulsive lying, and manipulation. For example, addiction to alcohol, drug, sex and other behaviors trigger the release of dopamine and other pleasure related neuro-chemicals into the brain. These substances make us feel good, and so we tend to go back for more. This leads to addiction – a form of control, enslavement and bondage.

John Calvin said "the human heart is a perpetual idol factory." The addictive substance such as alcohol or drug can be used as an idol to fill the holes in one's identity and self-worth. Addiction is a deadly idol that ends up taking control over us.

The Bible equates addiction to idolatry (Ezekiel 14:3). An idol is an object of extreme devotion. Addiction replaces the true invisible divine reality with a corrupted visible physical reality and eventually it takes control of us. Idolatry occurs every time the truth about God is exchanged for a lie, because idolatry is the worship of a created reality, instead of the Creator (Romans 1:25). To recover from addiction, an addict has to replace the substance of addiction with something else, such as worship, prayer, meditation, solitude, and service.

Addiction blinds us physically, emotionally, mentally and spiritually. In the physical, emotional and mental realm, addiction can treated as a disease that requires treatment. In the spiritual realm, addiction binds the mind, heart, and spirit and puts us in chains.

Why do we have to be concerned about Addictions?

- **Addiction Enslaves**
  Addiction is not just about what is done outwardly, but what we do about it inwardly. Jesus said that nothing outside a person can make them 'unclean' by going into the person. Rather, it is what comes out of the human heart that make them 'unclean' (Mark 7:19-20). Addictive behavior is a problem of the soul. For example, the addictive substance such as alcohol or drugs can be used as an idol to fill the holes in our identity and self-worth. However, addiction is a deadly idol that ends up taking control over us.

  Breaking away from addiction helps us to find our true selves. Instead of seeking who we are in the wrong places, Jesus can help us discover who we really are. C.S. wrote, "The more we let God take us over, the more truly ourselves we become... because He made us. He invented us. He invented all the different people that you and I were intended to be … It is when I turn to Christ, when I give up myself to His personality, that I first begin to have a real personality of my own." (C.S. Lewis, *Mere Christianity*)

How do we fight Addictions?

Addiction is a form of voluntary slavery. The Biblical approach to change or fighting addiction focuses on someone other than ourselves. Change begins, progresses and ends with Jesus. We must look to God's truth and away from ourselves (Mathew 11:28-29).

Here are some ways to fight addictions in the Bible:

- **Replacing the idols**
  An idol is an object of extreme devotion. The idols of the heart are like addictions such as alcohol or drugs that destroy (Ezekiel 14:3). As an idol, addictions end up having control over us. To replace the idols of the heart means to replace the corrupted physical reality with the true divine reality. Idolatry occurs every time the truth about God is exchanged for a lie, because idolatry is the worship of a created reality that is based on deception and lies (Romans 1:25). To recover from addiction, the addict has to worship something else that is more satisfying than the addictive substance – God. Change must target the heart, not just the behavior (1 Peter 2:11).

- **Saying No**
  Addictions are closely aligned with lies and deception. The Bible teaches that truth is the cornerstone of a good life. Speaking the truth imitates God's character, and lies violate God's character. In his book Confessions, Augustine speaks of how he struggled to say no to the chains of sexual addiction and drunkenness until a turning point came from reading the Bible. Augustine states: "I opened the Scriptures and read in

silence the passage on which my eyes first lighted: not in dissipation (self-indulgence) and drunkenness, nor in drunken revelry and sexual promiscuity, nor in arguing and jealousy; but put on the Lord Jesus Christ, and make no provision for the flesh or the gratification of your desires (Romans 13:13-14). I had no wish to read further, nor was there a need. No sooner had I reached the end of the verse than the light of certainty flooded my heart and all dark shades of doubt fled away (Augustine, *The Confessions*, Book VIII)."

- **Replacing Unhealthy Habits with Healthy Habits**
  To overcome addiction of any kind, we must focus on the habits and emotions that precede the addiction, as opposed to the addiction itself. There are emotional and mental habits that trigger the response of the addict. When deceptive and unhealthy thoughts arise, we must replace them with God's truth. As the good comes, the bad will become less attractive. God's plan is to strengthen the well-being of the whole person and bring goodness in every part of our life (Jeremiah 29:11).

In closing, Augustine of Hippo captures the control that the addiction of lust had upon him in the following words:

"Bound as I was, not with another man's irons, but by my own iron will. My will the enemy held, and thence had made a chain for me, and bound me. For of a froward will, was lust made; and a lust served, became custom; and custom not registered became necessity. By which links, as it were, joined together (whence I called it a chain) a hard bondage held me enthralled" (Augustine, *The Confessions*, Book VIII).

When
there is
enough evidence
to doubt what
is perceived
to be the truth,
will you still
hold firmly
to what
you believe
or would
you seek to
find the truth?

Chapter 19

The Problem of Delusion

Delusion: something that is falsely believed to be true or real, unreal
Deceit: the quality of being dishonest or misleading

Delusion is the inability to distinguish between what is real and what only seems to be real. A person with delusion will hold firmly to their belief even when there is evidence to doubt its truthfulness. For example, they may think that God is 'out there' in the external world while he is 'down here' within the human heart, mind and soul.

Delusion is not the same as deceit. Delusion is an idea or belief that is falsely believed by the mind as truth. Therefore, we act upon it. For example, it is delusional to connect drinking alcohol to having a good time. Deceit is an idea or belief that is wrongly perceived or interpreted by the senses. In deceit, the mind believes it is seeing the truth and will do anything to preserve this illusion. For example, the deceit in alcohol is hiding its negative consequences and luring its victim back.

The act of delusion is hiding the truth from yourself while deceit is hiding the truth from others. Regarding deceit, Jesus said, "If, therefore, the light that is in you is darkness, how great is that darkness" (Matthew 6:23). Jesus was saying that if the heart, the mind, reason and emotion are blinded by delusion, we will be lacking in our perception of the truth.

Delusional ideas and beliefs are very harmful not only by causing physical harm but by blinding us to the truth. Reason, emotions and will-power are powerless against delusional thoughts. Delusions can be a symptom of a medical, neurological, mental, or even spiritual condition.

The Bible says that Satan deceives, and by deceiving, he destroys (John 8:44). The Bible considers delusion to be a state of deception such as in the Garden of Eden, where Satan disguises as a talking serpent and deceives Eve. The main purpose of Satan's delusion is to mislead or destroy God's creation.

In the Old Testament, we read that Samson was deluded into thinking that he could get out of any situation. In his case, he was deceived because of lust. Deceit is hiding the truth from others, while delusion is hiding the truth from yourself. Samson hid things from God and his parents (Judges 14-16). Samson was delusional into thinking that the lustful pleasures will satisfy, forgetting the pain that follows.

Who is Deluded?
Anyone can be deluded, misled or deceived by others when they lack awareness of the truth. False beliefs can become normalized through the pressure of peer groups and social media. To overcome delusion, the Bible asks that we pay close attention to our inner self, our personal growth, and truth (1 Timothy 4:16).

Why is Delusion Dangerous?
Sooner or later, delusion leads to destruction because it is built on lies as opposed to truth. We are easily tricked into delusion by unconsciously believing lies which lead to self-destruction. Addiction may look attractive, but it is delusional because it is hiding the truth from yourself (Hebrews 3:13). Addiction is deceitful because it hides the pain that always follows.

The problem of delusion.

In his book '*The Screwtape Letters*,' C. S. Lewis gives plenty of examples of ways evil presents itself as desirable. For example, making sure that the patient (believer in Christ) spends plenty of time with materialistic friends, keep the patient from thinking too deeply about any spiritual matter, using everyday distraction to mislead the believer, cause the believer to become disillusioned with the church, and slowly deteriorate relationships.

How Can We Fight Against Delusion?
The Bible says that every thought and idea must be questioned if it is not to turn into something delusional.

Guard the Intellect and Heart
Anything new must be questioned against the Scripture. Whatever thought we allow to enter into our heart and intellect, will enter our spirit as a delusion if it is not examined properly (Proverbs 4:23). For example, in the garden of Eden, the 'forbidden fruit' stimulated the emotions of the heart (a delight to the eyes), and appealed to the intellect (desire to make us wise).

Value history and learn from it
History is the study of past events. Without the historical context, we will fall for every new idea or belief and become delusional. We are to remember the past, but not be held captive by it. Likewise, we are to remember divine providence and intervention in the past because they are expressions of our continuous relationship with God.

Divine providence in the past is meant to shape our identity as individuals by providing a baseline for everything that we stand for in life (Revelations 2:5, Deuteronomy 8:2).

Find meaning in your Destiny
To know meaning is the foundation of our existence. The Bible

says that we can find meaning because we are made in God's image (Genesis 1:26) and that we are good and responsible participants in God's creation – these facts have significance to the meaning of life because

- God made us a social creature (Genesis 2:18–25)
- God gave us work to do (Genesis 2:15)
- God wants to have a relationship with us (Genesis 3:8) and
- God gave us a free will to make good choices (Genesis 1:26).

The best antidote to delusion is to follow your destiny. Destiny is not something you do, but is something you are. It's more about who you become as you discover who God created you to be.

Are you
zealous
for God?
Is your zeal
single-minded
in focus?
Are you willing
to step out
for God?

Chapter 20

Zeal: Single-Minded Focus

Zeal: eagerness and wholehearted interest in pursuit of something
Zealous: passionate support for a person, cause, or ideal
Zealot: a person who is intensely or excessively devoted to a cause

Zeal is a strong feeling of enthusiasm or eagerness toward a particular cause. To have zeal is a positive and admirable quality that can inspire others to take action and make a difference. As a quality, zeal is being single-minded in one's focus.

Other words to describe zeal include single-mindedness, diligence, fervor, or to be zoned-in on your goal. Zeal is a warning against getting too comfortable, shallow or lethargic. The opposite of zeal is apathy, indifference or laziness.

Zeal is not to be confused with a zealot, a person who is fanatical in pursuit of one's religious, political, or other ideals. Ironically, the zeal of the Pharisees for the law caused them to become focused on rituals and keeping the law externally. They abandoned faith that comes from the heart and maintained outward pseudo spirituality (Matthew 23:23).

Zeal is derived from the Greek word 'Zelus', which personifies dedication, emulation, eager rivalry, envy, and jealousy. To be zealous means to burn with zeal toward a person or thing.

In the Bible, zeal is both commended and commanded. For example, Elijah had single-minded zeal in his commitment to God and his burning desire to see people worship God alone.

A classic description of zeal for God was given by J.C. Ryle. "He or she only sees one thing; and that one thing is to please God. Whether one lives, or whether one dies — whether one has health or whether one has sickness — whether one is rich, or whether one is poor — whether one pleases man, or whether one gives offense — whether one is though wise, or whether one is though foolish...for all this the zealous man cares nothing at all. If one cannot preach, work, and give money, one will cry, and sigh, and pray." (J.C. Ryle, *Practical Religion*)

Why do we need Zeal?

- Zeal is important because it keeps us running and moving forward.
- Zeal belongs to those who are fixated on principles, and are grounded in their faith, and therefore are strong, and do great exploits.
- Zeal is an attribute of God. For example, Jesus was filled with zeal for God's temple as a place of worship and not a place of business (John 2:17). The temple symbolized God's cause, His kingdom, and His glory.
- Zeal motivates, drives, and energize us. Never be lacking in zeal, but keep your spiritual fervor, serving the Lord (Romans 12:11).
- Zeal is rooted in knowing that we are loved by God.
- Zeal is being fearless for God, while staying focused upon God.

The prohibition of idolatry in the ten commandments tells us that we must have zeal for God alone, His honor and His cause. It is also called "jealousy for God."

How do we Cultivate Zeal?

- **Zeal takes Action**
  Instead of sitting back and waiting for heavenly intervention, we are to take the initiative for spiritual devotion and zeal. When Jesus saw the temple used for business (selling cattle and exchanging money), He was the only one who had the zeal to actually do something and take action (John 2: 13-16). Not taking action, delaying action, and neglecting our duty for action can be fatal(Joshua 18:3).For example, we have to develop a mindset that is habitually 'on fire' for Jesus, not just occasionally. To be lukewarm is to be slacking(Revelations 3:19).

- **Zeal takes Single-Minded Focus**
  Jesus said, "My food is to do the will of him who sent me and to finish his work" (John 4:34). Having single-minded zeal allows us to overcome obstacles and setbacks that might otherwise hinder progress (Acts 20:24). Zeal that is single-minded is not easily entangled in non-essentials. Zeal maintains focus, motivation, and resilience. The Bible compares zeal to a fire that is shut up on our bones (Jeremiah 20:9). The burning desire is to please God, to do His will, and to advance his kingdom in the world in every way possible.

- **Zeal takes Responsibility**
  In the Bible, God demands responsible action as an essential aspect of a faith. Staying full of zeal first begins by accepting the truth that zeal really matters (Romans 12:11). It is our responsibility to live our lives with eagerness and spiritual

devotion. The Bible emphasizes that a person who is responsible in little things, will be faithful in much, and so much is given to that person (Luke 19).

Dietrich Bonhoeffer is well known for his book, *The cost of Discipleship*, in which he rebuked Christians for following a shallow Christianity based on cheap grace, which is grace without discipleship, grace without Jesus Christ and the cross. He chose costly grace because it must be sought again and again. It is costly because it condemns sin, and grace because it justifies the sinner.

Bonhoeffer was daring and zealous for his faith. He was never afraid to stand up and speak boldly for his faith. Even though he had the opportunity to remain safe in the United States of America, Bonhoeffer chose costly grace and returned to his own country in a time of war. His faith was in doing, and having consequences. He wrote: 'When Christ calls a man, he bids him come and die'. He was hanged on 9th April 1945, just weeks before freedom arrived. His last recorded words were, 'This is the end - for me the beginning of life'.

PROCESSES

The processes are a series of actions
and guidelines that make us more
effective in our way of living,
thinking and feeling.

Did you
know that
God has a
personal and
eternal destiny
for you?
You can
choose to
accept it
or reject it
by the choices
you make.

Chapter 21

Destiny: A Pattern for Living

Destiny: something to which a person or thing is destined; a great or noble end

Destiny is what we are best cut out for in life. It gives a purpose, meaning, hope, joy and satisfaction. Neither fate nor human merit determines our destiny. The word 'destiny' is taken from the Latin root word destinare, which means to completely stand on purpose.

In Hebrew, to have a destiny is to have a vision or mission for one's life. Destiny has a negative connotation as in our fate and positive connotation as in our sense of mission. Moving towards our destiny is active, not something that is going to happen, but is a point towards which we are moving.

Destiny is not the same as fate. Fate means a predetermined state or end. With destiny, we have a choice on whether or not to discover and follow our destiny. God's destiny for us involves our full and willing cooperation. We have a free will to choose our own path.

In the Bible, destiny is used in the active sense of fulfilling God's purpose for our life in our generation (Acts 13:36). To fulfill God's purpose, we must connect with God in our thoughts, attitudes, choices, actions, and behavior. We cannot connect with our destiny without connecting with God. "Before I formed you in the womb I knew you, before you were born I set you apart" (Jeremiah 1:5).

131

The night before Jesus died, he claimed, "I have finished the work which you gave me to do" (John 17:4, Genesis 2:2).

Our identity leads to our destiny. First, through faith in Jesus Christ, we reach our eternal destiny (John 17:3). Since we are made in the image of God, our identity is in Christ (Psalm 16:5), not in an institution, ideology, past events, a person or thing. Second, each one of us is given certain talents, abilities, and experiences, which we are to use for good works. We are God's workmanship, created in 'Christ Jesus' to do good works. Third, good works, propelled by active faith, leads us to our destiny.

By applying God's truth to our life, propelled by faith, we reach our personal destiny (James 2:14). The reality of our relationship with God depends on the action that result from faith in Christ (John 15:16-17). Faith without works is dead and has no value.

Why is Destiny important?
Finding our destiny is not an easy path. It can be filled with challenges. It is possible to be distracted from our destiny. For example, we can encounter destiny destroyers which take us off the path of our destiny. For example, addiction to alcohol, drugs, toxic relationships, wealth, power, negativity, bad habits, and bad choices can hinder us from finding our destiny.

Without a destiny, we will feel empty and frustrated. Destiny is not just about the destination; it is also about the journey. When the Israelites were in the wilderness, God promised to dwell among them, and walk with them while they journeyed to the Promised Land (Leviticus 26:11-12). Destiny is God being present in our journey.

His plan requires of us a journey, illustrated so well in Bunyan's The Pilgrim's Progress, and that journey may be filled with

132

detours, sudden stops, and confusing turns. But if our hearts are set to obey Him in all that we know to do, then we will be in the center of His will every step of the way.

Destiny gives confidence to keep moving forward in life. God prepares us for our destiny through the positive, negative, and bitter experiences of life (Romans 8:28-30). Our journey is filled with detours, sudden stops, bumps, twists and turns. God will use each and every one of our experiences to fulfill our destiny. God can also use our bad experiences such as mistakes, traumas, and disasters as tools to fulfill our destiny.

How to arrive at one's Destiny?

To arrive at our destiny is to have an understanding of what our 'destiny' is. We cannot realize or materialize what we don't know. Faith with good works, in the active sense of the word is key to realize our destiny. We have a personal destiny to guide us toward a goal and plan our path forward. For example, the Bible says that after doing God's will for his generation, David died (Acts 13:36). Our eternal destiny is to have a relationship with God, in whose image we are made (Ezekiel 37:27). If we reject this relationship with God, our eternal destiny will be an eternal separation from God.

Here are some pointers to pursue our destiny:

Meaning and purpose in Destiny

Destiny is not something that we do, it is something we are. It is about who we become as we discover who God created us to be. To know meaning is the foundation of our existence. To know the 'why' is fundamental to reconstructing our meaning and purpose in life. We can find meaning in our relationships, career, family, work, faith and wealth. The Bible says that we can find meaning because we are made in God's image (Genesis 1:26) and because we are good and responsible participants in God's creation.

Here is a breakdown of what it means to be made in God's image:
- God made us a social creature (Genesis 2:18–25)
- God gave us work to do (Genesis 2:15)
- God wants to have a relationship with us (Genesis 3:8) and
- God gave us a free will to make good choices (Genesis 1:26).

Destiny Helpers

A destiny helper is someone who is connected to your destiny from a spiritual standpoint. For example, David and Jonathan, Moses and Aaron, Joseph and the Jailer. God brings 'Destiny Helpers' to guide us in our journey. These can be people, angels and even ravens to help us at critical times. For example, David's greatness would not be revealed if there was no Goliath. Goliath was a destiny helper for David. In the same way, Pharaoh's daughter was a destiny helper to preserve Moses, based on Pharoah's decree to have all male babies to be killed.

There will be destiny destroyers along the way. It is important to recognize our destiny helpers along the journey. The Bible says that our enemy, Satan is working very hard to distract us from our destiny (1 Peter 5:8). The Bible promises that God's truth will lead us to our personal and eternal destiny. We desperately need God; we are not capable of achieving our eternal and personal destiny without God.

Choices and Decisions

The kind of choices and decisions we make will lead us down the path to a certain kind of destiny. For example, we can choose to be bitter or to let go of the bitterness of the past. We must be fully invested in the destiny and withdraw from activities that drain one's destiny such as destructive thoughts, habits, addictions and toxic relationships (Galatians 5:16-26). Each of us at each moment is progressing toward our destiny or away from our destiny. Living life God's way gets you to the destiny He has.

We are exposed
to so much
negativity in
our lives and
the only way
we can flush
it out is by
renewing our
heart and mind.
But are you
willing to do
what it takes
to transform
yourself?

Chapter 22

Positive or Negative Exposure-Infection or Transformation?

Exposure: the fact or condition of being exposed, unprotected or at risk

Avoid the infection. In nature, a virus is a microscopic infectious agent that replicates itself within the cells of a living host. A virus needs a 'host' in order to spread. Once inside, the virus uses a type of protein to detect suitable host cells to infect. When a cell is infected, the virus duplicates itself within the host cell. It then breaks free from the cell and spreads throughout the body, infecting other cells. The role of the body's immune system is to fight and eliminate the virus from the body.

Negative exposure leads to infection. All living things interact with other living and non-living things in the environment to cause effects. The inter-connectedness is fundamental to life. We can catch infections through negative exposure to viruses in physical, mental and spiritual realms. Exposure to the spiritual virus can be harmful or detrimental through our thoughts, choices, actions, habits, behavior, and feelings. Examples of negative exposure to infections for mental health include bitterness, resentment, anxiety, fear, desire, and addictive behaviors.

Just as negative exposure leads to infection, positive exposure leads to transformation and renewal in physical and mental body. Positive exposures include generosity, kindness, justice, mercy, laughter, courage, self-control and other virtues. For example, our eternal destiny is to have a relationship with God, in whose image we are made (Ezekiel 37:27). If we reject this relationship with God, our eternal destiny will be an eternal separation from God.

God created us with a free will to choose between negative and positive exposure. That means we can choose to do good or bad, right or wrong. However, having 'free will' does not mean that we can do whatever we want without suffering the consequences. Even though we have free will, we are still responsible for the consequences of choices that we make. "For whatever a person sows, that they will also reap" (Galatians 6:7). We can choose to sow whatever we want, but we cannot choose what we will reap.

Negative Exposure and Infection
The choices we make and the eventual consequences of 'free will' make us vulnerable as a 'host' for the infection(Ephesians 2:2). Evil is like a parasite, it is a created being, not an original thing. Satan is a parasite who hunts for those who are most vulnerable to be a suitable "host" (Matthew 12:43-45).

A virus needs a host in order to spread and infect our body and mind. It can be a physical virus or spiritual virus - thoughts, choices, actions, behaviors, experiences and feelings. If the virus is successful, it will incubate and grow within our body and mind, then make us stray us off the correct path. Spiritual viruses poison our thinking through attitudes of bitterness, envy, jealousy, rebellion, and deception to get us off the path and cut us off from God.

Unless we repent, the negative infection will lead to even more infection. Sooner or later, the infected 'host' will pass the infection to others it comes in contact with. The risk of becoming infected is that we will waste valuable time and energy around the infectors, leading to misfortune and disaster. Many things are believed to be infectious, not just sickness. For example, unchecked freedom can lead to pride and destruction (Mark 7:22).

Jesus said, 'Take heed and beware of the leaven of the Pharisees and Sadducees' (Matthew 16:6-12). As a raising agent, yeast or leaven helps to puff up bread whereas unleavened bread is like flat bread, which is dense and thin, with no gaps or air, without corruption. Spiritually, leaven or yeast means 'corruption' not only of false doctrine, but of the corruption of sin. For example, malice which is the desire to cause pain, injury, or distress to another is the 'leaven' which corrupts the pure unleavened whole.

How do we overcome Spiritual Infection?

Healing from infection begins with diagnosis. The most dangerous injury is one where you do not recognize how serious it is. We may know that something is wrong with our body but postpone going to the doctor for diagnosis. Avoiding diagnosis can be deadly. The infection can destroy the cells and turn fatal. Early diagnosis can save your life, and this concept also applies for physical, mental and spiritual infections.

Here are some ways to fight spiritual infections:

• To overcome infections we must be quarantining in a place of isolation in which people that may have been exposed to infectious disease are placed. We isolate ourselves from the exposure to infections. Isolation keeps someone who is infected with the virus away from others. Isolation is an escape. "You will know the truth and the truth will set you free" (John 8:32).

- To fight infection, we must strengthen the body's immune system. In the spiritual realm, through the indwelling holyspirit, we can fight the infections in the spiritual body. We are to be vigilant, and on guard. "Be alert and thoughtful (clear-headed). Your enemy the devil prowls around like a roaring lion looking for someone to devour" (1 Peter 5:8).

- We need knowledge to treat the infection correctly. A lack of knowledge can get us into a lot of trouble. Isaiah 5:13 says, "My people go into exile for their lack of knowledge." Being infected with a spiritual virus is like being in exile. We are called to freedom, not to be exiled.

Positive Exposure and Transformation

Positive exposure leads to transformation and renewal that are contagious to the body, mind and spirit. It affects our attitudes, thoughts, feeling and behavior (Acts 11:19-30). Just as my qualities are passed on to my children, similarly, the attributes of God such as joy, peace, life, hope, rest, quiet confidence are passed on to us when we believe and accept God's truth. We cannot have these qualities without having Christ.

Asking for joy outside of a relationship with God is like wanting to be warm in the rain. We accept that cold is a quality of rain and that rain does not exist apart from cold. Similarly, to think that we can have good and desirable things apart from God is false (Genesis 3:5). Joy is a quality that does not exist apart from God.

How do we Cultivate Transformation?

Jesus came to this world and became a man in order to expose men and women to the transformed life that he offers. Transformation is a continual process, made possible by the renewing of our mind (Romans 12:2). Our mind is renewed by applying the Word of God to those things that will transform it.

We take on the mind of Christ by opening the secret and secluded parts of our inner being to Christ and fill it with God's truth and the Word (1 Corinthians 2:11–16). To have the mind of Christ, we don't merely use will power to think Christ's thoughts, we will ourselves to allow Jesus to live in our heart and mind.

Here is a comparison of negative and positive exposure:

Negative exposure: Infection	Positive exposure: Transformation
Resentment and bitterness are like a highly contagious viral infection in the mind, heart, and will.	Love, joy, peace, courage, kindness, gentleness, courage, and self-control are infectious characteristics in the mind, heart, and will.
Unresolved, negative feelings attach themselves to the mind like parasites and take up more and more of our time and energy.	People who have a positive outlook on life, and are not afraid to tackle difficult tasks inspire us to improve and achieve higher goals in life.
To persistently hold on to bitterness in the mind is to keep on confessing someone else's wrong.	When we befriend these kinds of people, we immunize and transform ourselves with the kind of character that produces good fruit in our life.

Is sloth
a problem
in one's spirit
or is it a
problem in
one's body?
Or is it an
aversion to the
good things
that God is
offering?

Chapter 23

Life in the Sloth Lane

Sloth: not inclined to action or labor; spiritual apathy and inactivity
Idle: not occupied or employed

The word 'sloth' is a translation of the Latin word acedia which means 'without care', originating from the Greek and Latin words for 'carelessness' and 'laziness'. Being slothful is laziness of the spirit or the 'whatever' mindset.

Being slothful is not the same as being 'idle', which is living in a carefree way or to waste, while sloth is slowness in the mind, when one is not inclined to action. The opposite of sloth is diligence or zeal. In the Greek, 'diligent' means to use speed, be prompt, to make effort, and be earnest. It means to exert oneself.

The Bible says, "The hand of the diligent will rule, but the slothful will be in bondage". In the Bible, sloth is a problem in one's spirit rather than the physical body. To be slothful is unique in that it is one of omission than commission; absence of a positive behavior than the presence of a negative behavior. Sloth is an aversion to the good things that God is offering and is usually rooted in the perception that inheriting these good things involves too much effort or sacrifice.

Soren Kierkegaard, a Danish Christian theologian saw busyness as a form of sloth, even though it seems like the other extreme of laziness. The reason is that both are vices. Busyness is a means of distracting our self and neglecting truly important questions, such as learning who we are, our eternity, destiny, death, enemy, and purpose in life.

Jesus came to give us a fulfilling and satisfying life, not a slothful one. Jesus spoke of the slothful servant who buried the talents entrusted to him by his Master (Matthew 25:14-30). God does not reward those with a slothful spirit (Joshua 17). Working hard is part of God's plan for our life. The Bible uses 'sloth' to describe King David's adultery and then the eventual murder. 'Spring' is a time when kings go off to war. David was relaxing and inactive when he should have been active on the job. As a result, David made himself vulnerable to sloth (2 Samuel 11).

Fighting the Demon of Sloth

Os Guinness writes, "What is undeniable is that when comforts and convenience sap our energies and idealism, inactivity secretes sloth in to our minds like a poison in the blood. Then as lethargy, tedium, and futility overtake us, we progressively lower our ideals and succumb. The result is sloth."

Sloth can affect us physically, mentally, emotionally, and spiritually. Physically sloth is a state of rest and indifference to work that expresses itself in the form of a lethargic mind. Emotionally, it is a lack of feeling for the world, or the people, or one self. Mentally, it leads to a sluggish state of mind by keeping us from paying attention to what is important.

Here are someways that sloth can emerge in our life:

- **Disconnect between Work and Career:** A disconnect between our God given 'calling' and our own career path may make us slothful. For example, when the work we do is directed by career goals alone, rather than being inspired by God's purpose for our life, our personal and eternal destiny.

- **Distorted Thinking:** Misuse of reason and distorted thinking can lead to self-deception. We deceive ourselves by thinking that we cannot deceive ourselves. Self-deception is a reality that can easily go undetected. Ultimately, reality is not negotiable.

- **Comfort:** A life of comfort and consumerism leads to ease and comfort and sloth draws near. True comfort rests in God (Psalm 16:2).

- **Loss of sense of worth:** More and more people today are unable to find life worthwhile. Our self-worth comes from being in the image of God, who has created us for good works (Ephesians 2:10).

How do we beat Sloth?

Sloth cannot be remedied with medicines but rather through spiritual healing. As physical and spiritual beings, we need a personal and eternal destiny. According to Dorothy Sayers, "Sloth is a sin which believes in nothing, cares for nothing, loves nothing, hates nothing, finds purpose in nothing, lives for nothing, and only remains alive because there is nothing it would die for."

Here are some ways to beat it:

- **Maintain focus:** The best way to counteract sloth is to purposefully stay focused, not allowing oneself to steer off the path. Without focusing on a unified purpose, one becomes 'double-minded', and distracted. Without guiding principles for life, we will fill up our time with busywork.

Be SMART

> **S: Specific -** Be specific about what needs to be accomplished. For example, memorize one Bible verse a week.
>
> **M: Measurable -** Making sure the goals are measurable makes it easier to track progress and know when you have reached the end goal. For example, memorize and write down one Bible verse each week.
>
> **A: Achievable -** Goals should be achievable and realistic, not so high that you inevitably tumble. Ask yourself: is your goal to memorize one Bible verse each week reasonable to accomplish?
>
> **R: Relevant -** Keep in mind the big picture. Why are you setting the goal that you are setting to memorize a Bible verse?
>
> **T: Time Limit -** To properly measure success, you need to know your time limit about when you will finish the goal to memorize one Bible verse each week.

- **Cultivate a growth mindset:** A growth mindset empowers us by making us believe that our abilities and habits can be cultivated, and are not static. This mindset leads to a different set of thoughts, and actions that we can employ to overcome challenges and use failures for growth.

A good example of growth mindset is the life of William Griffith Wilson, also known as Bill Wilson, who was a hopeless addict to alcohol. While lying in bed depressed and despairing, he cried out, I'll do anything! Anything at all! If there be a God, let Him show Himself! God did reveal himself to Bill, and he placed his faith in Jesus Christ. His life was utterly changed and transformed through spiritual experience followed by lifelong sobriety. He never drank gain and for the rest of his life, helped other alcoholics to stop drinking and eventually became the co-founder of Alcoholics Anonymous (AA).

Are you
the kind of
person who
will stop
at nothing
in your fight
for what you
believe in or
fight for truth
to prevail?

Chapter 24

Perseverance, Grit and Faith!

Perseverance: the quality that allows someone to continue trying to do something even though it is difficult
Grit: the strength of mind that enables a person to endure pain or hardship

A good example of a life of perseverance is Martin Luther, a German law student who was a monk turned theologian, and was the catalyst for the Protestant Reformation. To raise money, the church began selling indulgences, which were promises to pay on demand the bearer, forgiveness of sin for oneself and one's relatives. Using Romans 3:24, Luther lashed out that the church had no right to sell God's redemption through indulgences.

Luther was very passionate about helping the common man and woman to read and hear the Word of God, and understand that salvation is a gift from God. Salvation is received through faith 'all are justified freely by His grace'. To make this possible, Luther translated the Bible from Latin, the language of the scholars and clergy, to the language of the common person in Germany. It took Luther a lot of perseverance to overcome the opposition from the church, which included death threats, being declared an outlaw, fleeing for his life, and losing all that he had to help the people who lived in fear.

- Grit is one of the manifestations of faith. What we see displayed in Luther is 'grit' in faith - having the sense of purpose to accomplish a future goal, through perseverance. Here, grit was based on faith in God's truth in the Word. The dictionary defines grit as firmness of character; someone who cannot be overcome or conquered.

- "Grit is the ability to persevere in pursuing a future goal over a long period of time and not giving up. It is having stamina. It's sticking with your future, day-in, day-out, not just for the week, not just for the month, but for years and working really hard to make that future a reality. Grit is living life like it's a marathon, not a sprint". (Angela Duckworth, *Grit: The Power Of Passion and Perseverance*)

- Grit is similar to the biblical quality of fortitude, the mental or emotional strength to have courage in the face of adversity.

- Grit in the spiritual realm, is not the same as the self-glorifying worldly grit. Biblical grit has, at its core, a faith that rests on the promises of God and therefore is full of hope (Romans 15:13). Worldly grit places confidence in the 'self', while spiritual grit places confidence in God. The self is limited and finite whereas God is unlimited and infinite in wisdom. Worldly grit can be earned, while spiritual grit cannot be earned. Spiritual grit is granted through grace and undeserved kindness to those who exercise faith (Romans 3:23).

Athletes and soldiers show grit and fortitude. They undergo and endure rigorous, sometimes even torturous routines in order to accomplish the long-term goal of being the best in the world. Grit defines them.

Why does Grit Matter in Faith?

- Grit in faith must transfer to grit in real life, with grit, a believer in Christ acquires the stamina to consistently stand firm, empowered by God. Jesus said, "By your endurance, empowered by the Holy Spirit, you will gain your lives" (Luke 21:19).

Just like our body is strengthened by vigorous exercise, our faith too is strengthened by adversity. Adversity produces grit in faith.

Grit matters because:
It is a symbol of character and courage.
Here is a comparison of what it means to have fortitude, grit, backbone, and guts:

- **Fortitude**: Mental or emotional strength that enables courage in the face of adversity. It emphasizes strength of mind and firmness of purpose and implies endurance.
- **Grit**: Strength and firmness of mind that enables a person to encounter danger or bear pain. It emphasizes the capacity to be strong in difficulties or hardships.
- **Backbone**: Resoluteness of character; it implies either the ability to stand up in the face of opposition for our principles or chosen objectives, or determination.
- **Guts**: Physical and mental vigor essential both in facing something which repels or frightens one, and in putting up with the hardships it imposes.

Grit matters because:
- It teaches us to embrace the challenges of life, to make our self better.
- It develops a growth mindset of learning and growing. Though we fall, we get up. It is the opposite to having a fixed or static mindset.
- It nurtures hope and a sense of purpose, instead of helplessness.
- It helps us master challenges.

Growing Grit: Confidence in God versus Confidence in our self!

"Whatever you do, work at it with your whole being, for the Lord and not for men" (Colossians 3:23). Grit is not a generic trait but rather one that is learned through adversity and hardship. Everyone is born with a certain amount of grit. Without perseverance, distractions will veer us off the course. Grit is strength of character.

We develop grit and fortitude when our actions are controlled by principles. The Bible teaches us to build our principles based on God's truth, following His commands and refusing to turn to the left or the right (Proverbs 4:27), and letting His Word be our guide (Psalm 119:105).

Spiritual Grit	Worldly Grit
Core beliefs are based on scripture	Lacking in core biblical beliefs
Unlimited confidence in God	Unlimited confidence on self
A gift to those exercising faith; cannot be earned	Can be earned
Do the right thing (Matthew 5:43-48)	Do whatever it takes, right or wrong; evil or good
Rooted, undivided, and connected in Christ(1 John 2:27)	Divided, detached, disconnected (Mathew 5:16)
Nurture hope in God- Hope is a powerful motivator to spiritual action. (1 John 3:2, 3)	Lacking hope in God (Romans 15:13), one's own honor and self

Spiritual Grit	Worldly Grit
Say no, to ungodliness and worldly passions. Live self-controlled and upright life (Titus 2:2)	Say yes, to ungodliness and worldly passions. Slave to illusions of pleasures, without self control (Titus 3:3)
Bounce back from setbacks because God upholds you Psalm 37:23-24	Bounce back from setbacks by "pulling yourself up by your bootstraps".
God does not label anyone as a failure; we don't need to do it alone	The world labels us as 'failure'. When defeated we have to do it alone

Is your
heart and
mind fixated
on God's
truth?
Or, do you
allow yourself
to be distracted
or diverted
from the truth?

Chapter 25

Diversions

Diversion: someone or something that provides amusement or enjoyment
Distraction: a state of mental uncertainty

We live in a time of endless distraction. As a society we love noise, pleasure, and movement. Solitude is incomprehensible and is seen as a punishment. We are constantly in a state of diversion. To divert is to deviate or turn away from a standard or principle.

The dictionary defines diversion as turning something aside from its course. It is an activity that diverts or amuses or stimulates the mind by turning aside one's attention. Not all diversions are bad. There are traffic diversions to reroute traffic. Diversions also just be a source of amusement, happiness, or distraction from misery.

The military uses diversion as a tactic to draw attention away from the real threat or action. For example, drawing the attention of the enemy from the main operation to block desired information. Diversions are distractions come from both external and internal sources. External sources include emotional or visual triggers, digital media, text messages and phone calls. Internal sources include emotional pain, worry, trauma, and hunger. Diversion interferes with our focus.

The opposite of diversion is to be single-minded in one's focus. The ability to focus all of one's attention on something and to conform with rules or standards.

The Bible teaches that diversion is a strategy used by the enemy. God's truth keeps us on the path to a good life both now and in the future. Satan uses lies and deception to divert us from the truth. Jesus said, blessed are the pure in heart, for they shall see God (Matthew 5:8). The word 'pure' means 'single' or 'focused'. To be pure in heart means to be single-minded.

To overcome diversion, God wants us to have an undivided heart, a singleness of heart and mind (Ezekiel 11:19). Our main goal is to cultivate a heart and mind that is fixated on pleasing God alone, and not allow our self to be diverted by passing pleasures (James 1:8, Hosea 10:2).

In the *Screwtape Letters*, C.S. Lewis narrates about a senior demon named Screwtape, who advises a younger and less experienced demon to do his best to divert the believer from doing what God wants them to do. He talks about things such as sex, love, pride, gluttony, and war, that Satan will send our way to prevent us from the 'right' thing, and keep us paying attention to the wrong things.

The aim is to steal a believer from God (2 Timothy 2:25-26). Screwtape writes, "the safest road to hell is the gradual one – the gentle slope, soft underfoot, without sudden turnings, without milestones, without signposts."

The Dangers of Diversion

The global outbreak of the corona virus pandemic has thrust us into many forms of digital diversion, and without much of the social drama and validation that energizes so much of our lives, we often find ourselves lacking in purpose.

As Stephen Covey puts it, "People are working harder than ever, but because they lack clarity and vision, they aren't getting very far. They, in essence, are pushing a rope with all of their might".

Diversion becomes a distraction and a problem when it distracts us from ourselves and our destiny. In the process of being addicted to diversions, we become restless people.

Pascal points out that we need diversions to avoid looking into our own emptiness. Through constant activity we try to avoid becoming miserable.

He states, "Unmasked diversion is an attempt to escape reality, and indication of something out of kilter in the human condition. An obsession with entertainment is more than silly or frivolous. It reveals a moral and spiritual malaise or illness. The post-modern person seeks diversion as an overstimulation - a desperate bid to elude mortality by keeping higher realities out of sight."

Another reason we are addicted to diversion is because of our physical, emotional and mental bankruptcy. We use diversions to cover our inner bankruptcy with outward pleasures and busyness.

Diversions and distractions keep us from taking the time to reflect on what life is, on happiness, health, death and disease. We find ourselves constantly distracted in our thoughts and amusements. Jesus promises freedom from this bankruptcy.

How to Overcome Diversions?

Here are some ways to overcome diversion:

- **Putting First Things First**
  Prioritize and achieve your most important goals instead of constantly reacting to urgencies that come and go.

- **Taking the time for Reflection**
  To overcome diversion, we learn to reflect on or ponder over something, by focusing our thoughts on it. To reflect, we need an undivided heart: a singleness of heart and mind that does

not allow itself to be distracted or diverted by passing pleasures (James1:8, Hosea 10:2).

- **Meditating on God's Truth**
  Meditating on the truth in God's Word transforms our inner disposition to remain stable even when our external circumstances change. For example, when we memorize scripture and meditate, we not only keep our thoughts in order, we can also recall it when we need it. The memorized Word is a place of rest for the soul.

- **Beginning with the End in Mind**
  To begin with the end in mind means to begin each activity, work, or experience with a clear vision of our desired destination, and then continue by pushing forward.

- **Having a Spirit Controlled Life**
  God created humans with a spirit, a soul, (intellect, mind, will), and body. To be controlled by the spirit means to be ruled by the things of the spirit such as self-control,gentleness, faithfulness, goodness, peace, and love (Galatians 5:19-21) instead of diversions of the body, mind, and heart such as anger, repressed emotions, bitterness, and unforgiveness.

We are created as body, soul, and spirit. God designed for the human spirit to be the dominant part of our being, to rule the soul and body. By design, the soul is an intermediary between the body and spirit. In the 'natural' state with our inherent sense of right and wrong, the soul (intellect, mind, free will) becomes dominant over the spirit and body. In the bodily or worldly state, the body becomes dominant over the soul and the spirit (Jessie Penn-Lewis, *Soul and Spirit*).

Do you
trust your own
judgement?
Or are you the
kind of person
who conveniently
lies to yourself?
Do you
believe in
something
that seems like
truth even when
you know
it is not?

Chapter 26

Self-Deception

Deception: the act of causing someone to accept as true or valid what is false or invalid
Self-deception: allowing yourself to believe something about yourself that is not true

Have you ever found yourself going with the flow, doing things that go against your principles, even though it leaves you feeling empty or ashamed? Or have you ever found yourself settling for less than your worth or lying to yourself that you're really happy, when the best you feel is empty or frozen?

The word deception comes from the Latin verb decipere, meaning 'to ensnare'. Self-deception is the act of intentionally convincing yourself of something you know to be untrue. It is more than a lie. It corrupts and distorts the fundamental instinct that guides us through the difficulties of life. If a person is truthful, they can rely on their judgement and instincts, but if you deceive yourself then you can no longer trust your own judgement.

Truth requires courage. By manipulating truth, we are misled by our own 'deluded heart', so much so that we easily fool ourselves. For example, we can be seduced into riches, lustful pleasures that involve deceit or evil in the name of fun. Overcoming self-deception requires truth. Jesus said "You will know the truth, and the truth will set you free" (John 8:32).

The Bible warns us to not let anyone take us captive through philosophy and empty deception, according the tradition of the world, as opposed to the truth in the Bible (Colossians 2:8). For example, one type of self-deception we engage in is to believe that our words do not matter. Those who do not keep a tight rein on their tongues deceive themselves (James 1:26).

What is wrong with Self-Deception?
The problem with self-deception is that it brings a false sense of well being, physical, mental and spiritual. We dupe ourselves to deceive others and it eventually leads to ruin. The Bible warns us to "test the spirits" (1 John 4:1) and beware of the wolves in sheep's clothing (Matthew 7:15).

Permitting a problem like self-deception to remain unchecked is that eventually you become your problem. There is danger in fooling yourself with lies. You are the easiest person to deceive. Once you fool yourself, it will be easy to fool others. To overcome this, we must invest in our life with things that last, like truth, honesty, and integrity as opposed to things that are momentary and passing.

In the beginning, self-deception begins with slavery to a lifestyle or activity which then compounds to deceiving yourself and eventually destroying yourself. In the beginning it is temporary satisfaction, eventually it damages, corrupts and destroys our soul.

Do not be deceived!
The Bible says that God's desire is to bring us out, to bring us in (Deuteronomy 6:23). In the Old Testament, God brought His people out of bondage into the "promised land". This equally applies God's power to bring us out of self-deception into God's promises. God does not merely want to "to bring us out". God has a plan "to bring us in" to his promises for our life. These promises take us to our personal and eternal destiny, which self-deception has stolen from us.

How do we Fix the Problem of Self-deception?

We can overcome self-deception by cultivating love for truth, and testing everything with the Scriptures. Our culture, profession, or social media may tell us that truth is relative, for each individual to make up their own truth, thus diminish God's truth. The Bible tells us that there is only one version of truth, and it comes from God.

Here are some ways to overcome self-deception.
- **Invest in Yourself:** The danger of self-deception is fooling ourselves with lies and self-deception. We have to be intentional about elevating and advancing the things and experiences we most value and remove everything that distracts us from them. By investing our life with things that have a lasting value, we will experience truth and freedom. Freedom comes through God's truth; bondage comes through falsifying truth. "Lead me in your truth and teach me, for you are the God of my salvation" (Psalm 25:5).

- **Solitude:** We are too busy to live emotionally and spiritually healthy lives. The noise and clutter in our busy life style creates barriers to pursue truth. Solitude is temporarily withdrawing to be alone or away from the distractions to refresh the soul. The period of solitude may last few minutes, days or weeks. Solitude is not the same as isolation. Solitude is engagement whereas isolation is escape. Solitude is about opening yourself inner self to God while isolation spells danger.

- **Honesty:** To overcome self-deception and rebuild our life, honesty is key. Honesty not only to others but also to ourselves. Don't lie to yourself. A person who lies to themselves will soon lose respect for others and themselves. Jesus said, I am the way, the truth, and the life. When we choose God's truth, we will stop deceiving ourselves and others. God's truth will empower us to reprogram our mind of the lies, deception, delusion, and dishonesty and replace them with integrity and honesty Zechariah 8:16).

Do you
have the
right balance
between
work and
rest?
Do you
work
too much or
do you not
work enough?

Chapter 27

Work and Rest

Work: to exert oneself physically or mentally especially in sustained effort for a purpose or under compulsion or necessity
Rest: to cease from action or motion; refrain from labor or exertion

Work and rest are God's gifts to humans. Naturally, having the right attitude toward them should be a priority. But sometimes it can be difficult to find the right balance between work and rest. We either work too much and get stressed, or we do not work enough, leading to complacency and boredom. For many, work has become associated with guilt, a sense of hurry and worry.

Work is very foundational to our life, it is a basic human need like food, rest, friendship, or sleep. We make ourselves useful through work and therefore without meaningful work we lose our sense of significance. Work is also one of the ways we discover who we are, our abilities, and our talents, which are a major component of our identity. Work thus becomes a medium through which we offer ourselves to God. That said, even though work brings meaning to one's life, it is not "the only" meaning of life. If we make any work the purpose of our life, even spiritual activities, we create an idol that rivals God.

The opposite of work is 'rest', freedom from work, toil, strain or activity. Rest is not necessarily the same as sitting in front of the television or laptop, or staring at each other. While activities like these may seem pleasurable on the surface, they don't really satisfy or rejuvenate a person in any true sense.

A body is at rest when it ceases to move. The mind is at rest when it ceases to be disturbed or agitated. The spirit is at rest when it is released from anxiety, worry, and insecurity. However, many of us live our entire life more like the sea, never truly at rest (James 1:6). Resting strengthens our identity and emphasizes the principles we value. It helps us find the essence of life and allows time for contemplation.

We must find our comfort zone, a place where we feel safe or at ease, without stress. The book of Genesis portrays God as the primary worker who worked for six days and rested on the seventh day. God's plan includes the cycle of work and rest. God rested, not because He was tired, but to set the standard for mankind to follow. Spiritual rest is offered to all and is freely available by grace through personal faith in Jesus Christ (Matthew 11:28-30).

The rest that God offers can only be received by faith. Faith creates spiritual rest by giving us assurance that our lives are meaningful in the eyes of God, and therefore we have reason to improve and develop ourselves through work!

Below are kinds of rest based on Hebrews 3-4.
- The Divine Rest (Heb 4:1-3, 10-11)
- The Creation Rest (Hebrews 4:4)
- The Sabbath Rest (Hebrews 4:4, 4:9)
- The Canaan Rest (Hebrews 4:8)
- The Redemptive Rest (Hebrews 4:10)
- The Eternal Rest (Hebrews 4:9)

(Walter Kaiser, *The Promise Theme and the Theology of Rest*)

Why Balance Work and Rest?
Work and rest go together. Work gives meaning to rest. If we remove work, rest becomes meaningless. And while work is

meaningful, it should not be viewed as an end in itself. Work alone cannot give meaning to our lives: it is a tool, a means to an end. Rest has the power to open our eyes to ultimate meaning and purpose in life.

The Bible teaches us that whatever we do must be for His glory (1 Corinthians 10:31). The term "glorify" means "to give an accurate representation." Therefore, whether we are working or resting, our actions should portray an accurate picture of God. This includes faithfulness, gentleness, self-control, goodness, love, peace in place of envy, drunkenness, selfish ambition, rage, jealousy, hatred, and idolatry (Galatians 5:19-21). We must find our comfort zone between work and rest.

Here are some pointers on work and rest:

- Work and rest help to establish a person's identity.
- We reveal through our choices, in work and rest, the kind of identity we are pursuing.
- Overvaluing or undervaluing work and rest will hide this identity.
- Work and rest allow learning, and growth; they allow us to restore and rediscover life.
- Rest provides an inward-calm, an attitude of the soul, mind and body.
- Work and rest help us to cultivate the physical, mental, social and spiritual aspects of our life.

How do we Find our Comfort Zone?
Jesus does not call us to leave our comfort zone, but rather to find it. There is virtue in work and rest, and we are called to use both wisely. Rest is synonymous with grace, which is never seized by force but is taken freely by faith. Christ offers this rest.

- **Take the Sabbath Rest**
  Sabbath rest helps us to get into God's rhythm for our life. This will help us to cultivate a spirit of restfulness in place of restlessness. The goal is to rest so that we stay connected to God and get back to what matters most to our life. Rest has meaning for the physical, emotional, and spiritual aspects of our life. In the Old Testament, we read of creation rest, and rest from bondage to the worldly empire. There is no rest for those in slavery. They are not granted a day-off, they work until they die. In the New Testament, Christ is our rest. When we follow Christ whole heartedly, we experience the 'rest' that God promised by faith (Deuteronomy 1:36, Matthew 11:28).

- **Eliminate Hurry**
  As we absorb into a culture of hurry and busyness, we have less time for God. Not only does this adversely affect our relationship with God, we also become more vulnerable to principles of the secular world. For example, the world would say slow is bad and fast is good. One way to eliminate hurry is by choosing simplicity in the way we spend our time, and money on the things that adds value and sparks joy in our life.

- **Turn Off Technology**
  Turn off technology, then substitute with activities that renew and rejuvenate. Consider alternatives like hiking, jogging, taking a walk or going on a trip, talking to a friend, and helping others. The digital culture has bombarded our minds with endless stimuli that keeps us constantly distracted. For example, instead of checking our phones immediately upon waking, we can take time for silence to engage with God's promises. Turn your wandering mind to a praying mind. Be patient, don't despair when your thoughts wander. Instead of restricting the thoughts, take up the thought that has strayed into your prayer.

Are you
feeling stuck
or are you
willing to
stretch?
Are you
someone who
makes a wish list
and stops with
that or do you
go beyond?

Chapter 28

Necessary Endings and New Beginnings

Ending: something that constitutes an end
Beginning: the point at which something begins

E ndings are a necessary part of life, yet we experience them with a sense of regret and sorrow. When a person does not see endings as a necessary step for something better, the better will never come to that person's career, relationships, personal life, and spiritual growth.

To get to a new level or step, something has to end. For example, to cultivate good routines and habits, we have to break bad routines. We let go of old habits to grow into new habits. We relinquish some practices to make space for the next one. We unplug from some commitments to begin a whole new way of living. For example, if a job is not satisfying, or a good fit, it is reasonable to end it for a new beginning.

Necessary endings are similar to pruning a tree, cutting off that which is not beneficial or fruitful, in order to promote new growth. Pruning a plant ends unhealthy growth and encourages healthy growth and flowering to its fullest potential. For example, if a job is not satisfying or a good fit, it is reasonable to end it for a new job.

171

Pruning is essential. For a Christian, pruning is not a punishment but a reward. Jesus said, "every branch in me that does not bear fruit he takes away, and every branch that continues to bear fruit, He repeatedly prunes, to bear more and much better fruit" (John 15:2).

Necessary endings bring a new point of view by allowing us to pro-actively correct the bad and broken things in our life in order to make room for the good and beneficial. Unless bad situations are resolved, good outcomes will not come. We live in a culture that is all about new beginnings by consuming things, material wealth and living life to its fullest. We can easily lose sight of necessary endings.

Endings can often seem like an enemy because they can be painful, yet they are not final. Necessary endings are like a door with passage to something else, something better. Through this door, the real story begins.

Jesus is that door. Through this door, the real story begins. Jesus came to end and destroy the works of evil (1John 3:8). He came to give us a new beginning through 'real' life that is eternal and abundant (John 10:10).

Feeling stuck? How do we gain a better perspective?
Without necessary endings and new beginning, we can easily get stuck in habits, or situations that are hurtful, toxic, and even harmful. Behaviors that create destructive patterns can hold us back and hinder our growth. Until we let go of things that are not good, we may not find what is good. Keep in mind that necessary ending has to happen first before the new beginning can because we all have fixed amount of time and energy for any given day.

Initiating necessary endings for certain habits will allow for other new habits to begin. Instead of feeling stuck, we will stretch and challenge ourselves to experience freedom. It is crucial to remember that there is divine providence in necessary endings and beginnings.

Below are examples of necessary endings and new beginnings:

Necessary Ending: Habits to end	New Beginnings: Habits to begin
Addicted to the phone, technology, alcohol or other substances	Staying focused and not deviating from things that promote growth and value
Exhibiting bad, toxic, and destructive habits, and relationships	Cultivate good habits, and relationships
Wandering mind filled with guilt, hurry, and worry	Staying grounded on the truth through prayer and the Word of God
Being selfish, stingy, and self-centered	Being generous in giving your time, possessions, money and abilities leads to vitality

How can we initiate necessary endings and new beginnings?
Here are some ways to initiate necessary endings and new beginnings.

- **Reset your Mindset:** A mindset is a set of attitudes, beliefs and thought patterns that shape our worldview. A faith-based mindset is built on a Biblical worldview, based on God's truth in the Word of God. We can set specific goals and create plans for necessary endings and new beginnings. For some things time has passed and therefore endings are necessary for growth. Be intentional about removing anything that competes and

173

prevents the new beginnings. It is critical to not give up on yourself. For example, write it down, talk about it and make it real (Habakkuk 2:2).

- **Feedback from Mentors:** It is crucial to find a mentor who can offer perspective and wisdom in the journey from necessary endings to new beginnings. Mentors help you navigate, answer questions and offer accountability. Moses was a mentor to Joshua, Elijah was a mentor to Elisha, and David was a mentor to Solomon.

- **Ending as a Necessary step:** We take bold steps to something better by seeing the ending as a necessary step, else we will stay stuck, never reaching our true potential (Numbers 13). We do so by moving beyond our fears, knowing that God has something good in the future, even though we may not see clearly what that might be. We put an end to darkness by bringing in light (Job 28:3).

In his book *Necessary Endings*, Henry Cloud says, "When truth presents itself, the wise person sees the light, takes it in, and makes adjustments."

In the Bible,
revelation is
the way in
which God
communicates
with us.
But are we
listening to
God's Word,
to see what
God is
revealing
to us?

Chapter 29

Decoding Revelation

Reveal: to make known through divine inspiration
Revelation: an act of revealing to view or making known

"Information may inform the mind, but revelation sets a heart on fire" (Matt Redman).

In Hebrew, revelation is the supernatural communication of truth to the mind. The Greek word for revelation is apokalypsis, which is to remove the veil in order for something to be seen.

The opposite of revelation is mystery, something that is unexplained or unknown. A revelation searches and calls out the deep and mysterious things. A mystery on the other hand is a truth that can be fully understand only by revelation.

In the Bible, a revelation is the way in which God communicates with us. We are responsible for listening to God's Word, to see what God is revealing to us. The Bible says, "The secret things belong to the LORD our God, but those things which are revealed belong to us and to our children forever, that we may do all the words of this law" (Deuteronomy 29:29). It is God's ability to 'reveal' things to come; we are encouraged to "do all the words of this law", not to diminish it in any way.

The outcome of a revelation is strength, empowerment and action (Revelation 1).

- Strengthen: to show something that was not known or seen, thus providing hope for today and the future.
- Empower: to enable and give someone authority and freedom to do the right thing.
- Act: to take action or do something in response to the revelation.

Revelation and Faith

Revelation and faith work together. Revelation is the basis of our faith. What is known by reason is knowledge, not faith. Faith assumes revelation. Revelation unveils the truth and the truth sets us free; it does not deceive us. A revelation motivates the believer to overcome (1John 5:4).

Jesus is the focal point of all revelation. Faith in Christ is by itself a revelation that allows us to operate differently in the world. We do not need to chase after revelation since we have already received a revelation in Christ.

How to Apply Revelation?

When John wrote the book of Revelation, he was exiled and banished to a small island in the Aegean Sea, which is a part of Greece today. To be 'exiled' means to send someone away from their own country. In Hebrew, 'exile' is a place of suffering. Even in exile, revelation provided divine guidance and inspiration to communicate truth and knowledge from God. When the revelation came, John was 'in the spirit', he was sensitive to the things of the 'spirit', not just the body (Revelation 1:10).

To receive divine revelation, we have to be 'in the Spirit', because God is spirit and those who worship Him do so in spirit and truth (John 4:24). To be in the spirit means to experience God inwardly, from the heart. God is not bound by space or time because He is infinite always. His worship is not confined by place or shape but by things that have meaning, significance and value.

Divine Revelation and Human Experience

As we read the Bible, we pick up some basic facts from the Bible. We need revelation about the basic facts that we read and this comes by exercising our human spirit. The more we exercise our spirit over the Word through study, prayer, meditation or reflection, the greater the revelation. As we repeatedly review the revelation from reading the Bible, light emerges on divine revelation and it gradually becomes a vision to us. The vision gives us the ability to see. The vision then begins to dominate our thinking and move us to action.

There is a worldly vision that bases itself on what it can see, touch, and feel as the only truth. Christianity is based on a spiritual vision.

"Christianity begins with a completely different base line and therefore judges everything differently. The reason it judges so differently is that it judges human experience by divine revelation, while the world judges divine revelation by human experience". Christianity sees the present experience of human behavior as abnormal, while the world judges this religion as abnormal. Each implicates the other's standard. (PeterKreeft, *Christianity for Modern Pagans: Pascal's Pensees*)

The Purpose of Revelation

Here are some reasons why God sends His people a revelation:

- **To Reveal Spiritual Warfare:** The human mind needs a revelation to see the truth and fight evil forces that terrify, oppress, and imprison us (Revelation 12).

- **To Reveal how to Optimize our Life:** By bringing a divine perspective to our life, a revelation allows us to optimize life, by patterning after God. For example, the world is capable of constantly pulling us downward whereas the Word of God is constantly pulling us upward (Ephesians 1:18).

- **To Bring Freedom:** Revelation brings freedom to our thinking, behavior, and lifestyle. Revelation removes fear about past, present and future events (2 Timothy 1:7).

- **To Empower:** God reveals through prophecy, spirit of discernment and visions to empower the believer and to overcome setbacks (Isaiah 40:5-7).

- **To Transform:** Revelation transforms our daily living by connecting the mind to the heart. We can spend our entire life time trying to connect our mind to our heart (Deuteronomy 6:5).

In closing, divine revelation is not something that we can prepare for with a strategy or plan. The highest revelation is that God dwells within each one of us (Revelation 21:3). The Bible itself is a revelation from the infinite God to finite humans.

There is
a saying,
"March to
a drumbeat
that you
believe in."
But the
question is,
to whose
drumbeat
are you
marching
to?

Chapter 30

Marching to which Drumbeat?

Marching: to move along steadily in step with others; to move in a direct purposeful manner

Whether we are aware or not, we all march to the drumbeat of someone or something, it can be social media, a friend, a spouse, a political party, or even our own drumbeat. Marching to our own drumbeat is the practice of marching in step to drum beats in military parades. In this context, someone who marches to their own drumbeat would be out of sync with the rest, indicating their failure or refusal to conform to an established rule or practice.

The question is not whether we march to a drumbeat, but whose drumbeat we march to. Is it God's or the worlds?

The Bible teaches us to march to God's drumbeat, even if it means that we are out of step with those around us. For example, the Bible teaches us to delight in righteousness, justice and mercy, because God delights in them. Righteousness means to act in accord with divine or moral law. However, when social culture is out of step with God's moral law, we must march to a different drumbeat - obeying God rather than culture.

In the Old Testament, Elijah proclaims, "As the Lord lives, before whom I stand" (1 Kings 17, 18, 2 Kings 5:15-16). In the Biblical Hebrew worldview, the key to achieving stability depends on the way in which we position our self with God. Standing before God means to be synchronized with God's laws or practices (Deuteronomy 29:9, Ephesians 6:13). This does not mean an intellectual synchronization. To stand before God and march to His drumbeat means:

- Being attentive to God's ways and rules.
- Being aware of our audience with God, and that other audiences do not matter.
- Understanding that there is nothing to prove to this world, except to Jesus Christ. There is nothing to gain or lose from the applause and approval of this world.
- Being inner-directed in thought and action using God's principles than by external norms such as social validation, friends, wealth, status, etc.

Why do we have to March to God's Drumbeat?

There is a saying, 'March to a drumbeat that you believe in.' Marching to God's drumbeat will change the rhythms of our life. Living according to God's rhythms will turn us into brave, courageous, credible, pleasant, healing, moral and truthful people.

By marching to God's drumbeat we are seeking God's approval instead of the approval or blame of friends or peers. George Muller states: "There was a day when I died; died to self, my opinions, preferences, tastes and will; died to the world, its approval or censure; died to the approval or blame even of my brethren or friends; and since then I have studied only to show myself approved unto God".

To March to God's Drumbeat (God's truth)	To March to the World's Drumbeat (World's Truth such as social media, friends, ideologies)
Single minded focus on walking with integrity before God	A divided heart, Fear of the world and God

To March to God's Drumbeat (God's truth)	To March to the World's Drumbeat (World's Truth such as social media, friends, ideologies)
Blessings come from marching to God's drum beat and being in step with God (Joshua 1:3)	Marching to a different drumbeat, not God's laws; Captive to flawed heroes
Repair, Restore and Rebuild (Amos 9:12)	Destroy, drain, exhaust, and weaken
No longer chained to self; Died to self (John 3:3)	Chained to self (2 Timothy 2:9)
Living out of convictions: strong and wise (Mathew 7:24 - 27)	Living according to people's wishes - foolish; become man's slave and nothing better

How do we March to God's Drumbeat?

Because Elijah took the time to stand before God, he was able to stand boldly before the king and the people. Elijah went before the people and said, "How long will you waver between two opinions? If the LORD is God, follow him; but if Baal is God, follow him." But the people said nothing (1 Kings 18:21). Here are some ways to march to God's drumbeat:

• **Be Inner Directed:** To be Inner-directed means to be directed in thought and action by God's values and laws, as opposed to external norms. Inner compass has to do with a person's inherent qualities of mind, heart, and character. This involves reflection, listen to our mind and heart, and examine our thoughts and feelings. For example, to be inner directed does not mean a simple reading of the Word of God. Instead, we are to read the Word of God, ponder over it, meditate upon it, memorize it and apply it to our life. Living by God's truth will propel us to be inner directed so that our inner disposition stays the same even when outward circumstances change.

- **Practice the Presence of God:** Practicing the presence of God is a spiritual discipline to apply the Word of God to the secret and secluded part of our inner being. God can be invited into everything we do and His presence can be enjoyed anytime. Even though practicing the presence of God is not as simple as it sounds, the challenge is to remain attentive and focus on maintaining God's presence.

  Brother Lawrence is known for his devotion and ability to bring God into every aspect of his life, cooking, cleaning, doing the dishes, etc. His work, Practice of the Presence of God, details how to gain that constant connection to God. This presence was maintained by love rather than understanding, speech, fear or judgement.

- **Escape Futility:** We cannot live a fulfilling life unless we replace futility with meaning and purpose in life. When we are spiritually lacking, we experience emptiness, and lack a sense of meaning and purpose, which leads us to seek other alternatives. For example, when life loses its meaning, some will turn to alcohol or other substances to escape the futility. From a Biblical perspective, each one of us has a divine a sense of meaning and purpose because:
  a) We are created in the image of God and
  b) God calls us into a relationship with Him. Discovering this purpose leads to growth in life and transformation.

In the end, whose drumbeat we are marching to is a call to finding our sense of purpose and fulfillment in Christ. Jesus said, "he who has ears to hear, let him hear" (Luke 8:8).

NOTES

This section includes a list of sources, citations, and references for each chapter in the book. It is my desire that readers will find this list useful. If I have inadvertently failed to give credit to someone where it is due or failed to attribute an idea to the right person, please email me at rajulajacobchandran@gmail.com

All definitions are taken from the Miriam Webster dictionary. All Bible references are taken from the Amplified, and New International Version of the Bible.

Chapter 1: The Creation Mandate

11 **Yearning to know what cannot be known**:
Aiden Wilson Tozer, *The Knowledge of the Holy* (New York: Harper and Row, 1985).

14 **Creation as a progression**:
David Parry, Milton and the Bible, Darkness Visible hosted by Christ's College at Cambridge University, 2008), https://darknessvisible.christs.cam.ac.uk/religion_bible.html.

Chapter 2: Logos Demystified

18 **The word:** Francis S. Collins, *The Language of God: A Scientist Presents Evidence for Belief* (New York: Free Press, 2006).

19 **Logos-word**: Lawrence A. Layton, *Martin Luther: Treatise on Good Works* (Alabama: Regimen Books, 2017).

20 **The Word and spirit**: Andrew Murray. *With Christ in the School of Prayer* (Middletown: Eternal Sun Books, 2016).

20 **To follow the Logos-Word**: Deitrich Bonhoeffer, *The Cost of Discipleship* (New York: Macmillan Publishing, 1937).

Chapter 3: Knowing God and known by God

22 **Knowing God**: C.S. Lewis, *They Asked For A Paper: Papers and Addresses* (London: Geoffrey Bles Ltd, 1962), 164-165.
24 **Belief in God**: C.S. Lewis, *Mere Christianity* (San Francisco: Harper One, 1952).
24 **Knowing God**: C. S. Lewis, **A Mind Awake: An Anthology of C. S. Lewis** (Boston: Houghton Mifflin Harcourt, 2003).
24 **Knowing God**: Alister E. McGrath, C.S. Lewis: *A Life* (Leicester: W F Howes Ltd 1953).
25 **Life becomes disappointing without knowing God**: John Bunyan, *Pilgrims Progress* (Connecticut: Macmillan and Co, 1905).
25 **Faith is God felt by the heart**: Blaise Pascal, *The Thoughts of Blaise Pascal* (Westport: Glenwood Press, 1978), 277, 278, 279.
26 **Spiritual disciplines**: Richard Foster, *Celebration of Discipline: The Path to Spiritual Growth* (New York: Harper and Row, 1978).

Chapter 4: Meaning of the Cross

30 **Meaning of the cross:** John R. W. Stott, *The Cross of Christ.* Downers Grove: InterVarsity Press, 2006.
31 **Divine love:** C. S. Lewis, *The Four Loves*, (Boston: Mariner Books, 1971).
32 **Lessons for a Christian to learn:** Handley Carr Glyn Moule, Charles Simeon (London: Methuen and Co, 1892).

Chapter 5: What is a Covenant

36 **Marriage as a covenant:** Dr. Tony Evans, *Kingdom Man* (Carol Stream: Tyndale House Publishers, 2015).
36 **The condition of the heart is critical:** Andrew Murray, *The Two Covenants* (Fort Washington: CLC Publications, 2005)

37 **Responsibility:** Viktor E. Frankl, *Man's Search for Meaning* (Boston: Beacon Press 2017).

Chapter 8 Cosmos or Kingdom of Heaven

53 **Kingdom of heaven is to overcome evil:** George Eldon Ladd - *Jesus and the Kingdom, The Eschatology of Biblical Realism* (London: Harper & Row Publishers, 1964).

Chapter 9 To Follow. To Pursue

57 **Hound of Heaven:** John Stott, *Why I am a Christian* (Illinois: Intervarsity Press, 2003).
58 **God instilled within us a desire for Him**: C.S. Lewis, *Mere Christianity* (New York: Touchstone, 1996).
59 **Heart is restless until it repose in Thee:** St. Augustine, *The Confessions* (London: Penguin Books 1961), Book 1, 2.

Chapter 10 Betrayal or Allegiance

64 **To move past the betrayals of life:** C.S. Lewis, *The Weight of Glory* (New York: Macmillan and Co., 1966).
64 **How to stop betrayals:** C.S. Lewis, *Mere Christianity* (New York: Touchstone, a division of Simon & Schuster, 1996).

Chapter 11 The Battle for Heart and Mind

70 **Heart and reason:** Blaise Pascal, *The Thoughts of Blaise Pascal* (Westport: Glenwood Press, 1978).
71 **Why the body, soul and spirit are significant:** Bibles for America, The 3 parts of man-Spirit, Soul and Body, June 22 2015, https://blog.biblesforamerica.org/the-three-parts-of-man-spirit-soul-and-body/
73 **Means of belief:** Blaise Pascal, Pascal's Pensées (New York: Bibliotech Press, 2023).

Chapter 13 The Power of Responsibility

81 **Responsibility:** Stephen R. Covey, *The 7 Habits of Highly Effective People* (New York: Free Press 2004).

83 **Expect great things, attempt great things:** Timothy George *Faithful witness: the life and mission of William Carey* Internet Archive: Christian History Institute in association with Samford University, 1998, Internet Archive archive.org

84 **Who we are and who we are becoming:** C.S. Lewis, *Mere Christianity* (New York: Touchstone, a division o & Schuster, 1996).

Chapter 14 Change your Perception, Change your Life

88 **Our perception creates our reality:** C.S. Lewis, *The Magicians Nephew* (Collier Books 1955), page 125.

90 **Knowing our enemy:** C.S. Lewis, *Paved with Good Intentions A Demon's Roadmap to your Soul* New York: Harper Collins 1996

90 **Martin Luther and the protestant reformation:** Boehmer, Heinrich *Martin Luther: Road to Reformation*, New York: Meridian Books 1957, pages 110-112. Internet Archive archive.org

Chapter 15 Prayer: The Discipline

93 **Prayer:** Foster, Richard J. *Celebration of Discipline.* San Fransisco: Harper, 2002.

94 **Means of belief:** Blaise Pascal, *Pascal's Pensées* (New York: Bibliotech Press, 2023).

94 **The human spirit:** Bibles for America, The 3 parts of man-Spirit, Soul and Body, June 22 2015 https://blog.biblesforamerica.org/the-three-parts-of-man-spirit-soul-and-body/

95 **Power of prayer:** Tony Evans, *Kingdom Man.* Illinois: Tyndale House Publishers, 2020, Chapter 2 The Covenant, page 11

96 **Union of Word and Spirit:** Andrew Murray, *With Christ in the School of Prayer* (New York: Fleming H Revell, 1885).

Chapter 16 Meditation: The Discipline

99 **Biblical meditation**: Foster, Richard J, Celebration of Discipline (San Fransisco: Harper, 2002).

102 **Meditation and practice**: Thomas J. Watson, *A Christian on the Mount* (Prescott, Ontario Canada West, 1862).

Chapter 17 The Power of New Affections

105 **New affections**: Thomas Chalmers, *The Works of Thomas Chalmers* (Glasglow: M. Sherman, 1829, Volume 1) Internet Archive archive.org

106 **Knowing God**: James Innell Packer, *Knowing God* (Illinois: Inter Varsity Press 1993).

Chapter 18 Addictions: Idols of the Heart

111 **Human heart as an idol factory**: John Calvin, *Sermons of John Calvin* (San Francisco: Internet Archive, 1580), https://archive.org/details/bim_early-english-books-1475-1640_sermons-of-maister-john-_calvin-john_1580/mode/2up?q=idol

112 **The human heart**: John Stott, *The contemporary Christian* (Leicester: Inter-Varsity Press, 1992).

112 **Finding our true selves**: C.S. Lewis, *Mere Christianity* (New York: Touchstone, 1996).

114 **Held hostage by lust**: St. Augustine, *The Confessions* (London: Penguin Books 1961), Book 8.

Chapter 19 The Problem of Delusion

119 **Why delusion is dangerous**: Alan Vermilye, *Screwtape Proposes a Toast Study Guide*, https://brownchairbooks.com

Chapter 20 Zeal: Single Minded Focus

124 **Zeal for God**: John Charles Ryle, *Holiness* (Welwyn Garden City: Evangelical Press, 2012), Internet Archive https://archive.org/details/holinessitsnatur0000ryle

126 **Zealous for faith in Christ**: Dietrich Bonhoeffer, *Letters and Papers from Prison* Edited by Eberhard Bethge (New York: The Macmillan Company, 1972, archive.org), https://archive.org/details/letterspapersfro0000bonh_d5e4/page/4/mode/2up?view=theater&q=single

Chapter 21 Destiny

132 **Why destiny is important**: John Bunyan, *The Pilgrim's Progress*, Carlisle, Pennsylvania: The Banner of Truth, 2017.

Chapter 22 Exposure and Transformation

138 **Infection and diagnosis**: C.S. Lewis, *Mere Christianity* (Harper One, 1952), 32.

Chapter 23 Life in the Sloth Lane

144 **Busyness as a form of sloth**: Soren Kierkegaard, *Practice in Christianity* (Princeton : Princeton University Press, 1991).

144 **Fighting sloth:** Os Guinness, *The Call: Finding and Fulfilling the Central Purpose of Your Life* (Nashville: Nelson Publishers, 2003).

146 **Cultivating a growth mindset**: Bill Wilson, *Alcoholics Anonymous: The Big Book Mineola*, Dover Publications, 1939.

Chapter 24 Perseverance, Grit, and Faith

149 **Perseverance, grit and faith**: Martin Luther: *Treatise on Good Works* (Northport: Regimen Books, 2017).

150 **Grit and faith**: Angela Duckworth, Grit: *The Power of Passion and Perseverance* New York: Scribner Publishing, 2016.

Chapter 25 Diversions

156 **To divert from doing what God wants you to do**: C.S. Lewis, *The Screwtape Letters* (San Francisco: HarperOne, 2001).

156 **Dangers of diversions**: Stephen R. Covey, *The 7 Habits of Highly Effective People* (New York: Free Press 2004).

157 **The misery of man without God**: Blaise Pascal, *Pascal's Pensées* (New York: Bibliotech Press, 2023).

158 **A spirit controlled life**: Jessie Penn-Lewis, *Soul and Spirit: Finding Freedom in Christ* (New Kensington: Whitaker House, 2012).

Chapter 26 Self Deception

163 **Solitude and isolation**: John Mark Comer, *The Ruthless Elimination of Hurry* (Colorado Springs, Waterbrook Publishers, 2019).

Chapter 27 Work and Rest

166 **Kinds of rest**: Walter C. Kaiser, Jr., *The Promise Theme and the Theology of Rest*, Bibliotheca Sacra Volume 130:518. April, 1973. https://web.archive.org/web/20130919060247/http://www.thepromise.typepad.com/197304.pdf

168 **Eliminate hurry**: John Mark Comer, *The Ruthless Elimination of Hurry*. Colorado Springs, Waterbrook Publishers, 2019.

Chapter 28 Necessary Endings and Beginnings

174 **Endings are a necessary part of life**: Henry Cloud, *Necessary Endings* (New York: Harper Business, 2011).

Chapter 29 Decoding Revelation

177 **Worship**: information and revelation: Matt Redman, Twitter
Post, November 15, 2010, https://twitter.com/matt_redman/
status/4404382938439680 In worship it's not what you know,
but who you know. Information may inform the mind, but
revelation sets a heart on fire.

179 **Christianity is based on a spiritual vision**: Peter Kreeft,
Christianity for Modern Pagans: Pascal's Pensées (San Francisco:
Ignatius Press, 1993).

Chapter 30 Marching to which Drumbeat?

184 **Marching to God's Drumbeat:** George Muller, London
Quarterly Review Volume 92.

186 **Practicing the presence of God**: Brother Lawrence,
The Practice of the Presence of God (New Kensington: Whitaker
House, 1982)

INDEX

Trust, 36, 61-62, 64, 71, 75, 140, 156-157

U

Understanding, 21, 67, 69, 87, 92, 129, 180, 182
Unique, 8, 9, 29, 30, 57, 139

V

Vision, 85, 104, 127, 152, 154, 175, 176
Vermilye, Alan, 117

W

Watson, Thomas, J., 100
Wilberforce, William, 55
Wilson, Bill, 142
Words, 16, 22, 45, 90, 93, 97, 99, 112, 121, 158, 173
Work and rest, 13, 164 -168
Worldview, 1, 2, 4, 14, 27, 28, 74, 87, 169, 180

Z

Zeal, 81, 120,123-124, 139
Zealous, 120-122, 124